MEMORYSCOPES

MEMORYSCOPES

REMNANTS FORENSICS AESTHETICS

ROSS GIBSON

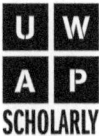

First published in 2015 by
UWA Publishing
Crawley, Western Australia 6009
www.uwap.uwa.edu.au

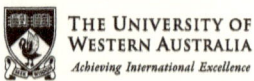

THE UNIVERSITY OF
WESTERN AUSTRALIA
Achieving International Excellence

This book is copyright. Apart from any fair dealing for the purpose of private study, research, criticism or review, as permitted under the *Copyright Act 1968*, no part may be reproduced by any process without written permission. Enquiries should be made to the publisher.

The moral right of the author has been asserted.

Copyright © Ross Gibson 2015

National Library of Australia Cataloguing-in-Publication entry

Creator: Gibson, Ross, 1956- author.

Title: Memoryscopes : remnants forensics aesthetics / Ross Gibson.

ISBN: 9781742587592 (paperback)

Subjects: Aesthetics.
    Art--Philosophy.
    Art appreciation.
    Art and history.
    Multimedia (Art)
    Interactive multimedia.

Dewey Number: 701.17

Typeset in Bembo by J&M Typesetting
Printed by Lightning Source

CONTENTS

Preface		vi
1	The Flood of Associations	1
2	Places Past Disappearance	13
3	Remembering a Future with Landscape	26
4	'All Things are in Contact': archives, memory, imagination	33
5	Extractive Realism	48
6	Spirit House	64
7	The Pulse in the Past	75
8	Aesthetics and Something More than Meaning in Forensic Photographic Evidence	89
9	Self Extraction	109
10	Where the Darkness Loiters	124
11	Palpable History	134
12	Politics, Poetics and Policing	146
13	*The Searchers* Dismantled	156
14	'Who Knows the Weather?': The Memory of Greg Dening	173

PREFACE

Memoryscopes is a companion to *Changescapes,* in which I pondered aesthetic forms and artistic means for understanding complexity and mutability in contemporary culture. In a related way, *Memoryscopes* has grown from my past couple of decades creating and analysing artworks built from traces that history has left lying around in archives, in landscapes, in objects, in peoples' bodies, in biographies and in family histories. This book is an examination of some particular modes of remembrance. It investigates aesthetic forms or 'memoryscopes' that we can reach for, if they have already been created, or that we might have to invent in order to contain, focus and direct the forces of the past.

A good memoryscope focuses the forces of the past so they can be comprehended and channelled in such a way that meanings and feelings implicit to the past might get effectively communicated to the people of the present, in a manner that is more than just *ad hoc* or random. I think of the work one can do with a memoryscope as a process that is simultaneously aesthetic and forensic. If this sounds a tad runic right now, the book will give some concrete heft to these abstract propositions as we go through the chapters.

Whereas *Changescapes* examined the dynamic *present* in which experiences are always altering systematically to become the next future moment, *Memoryscopes* examines how *the past* has dynamism too, how it is a force always pushing and skewing the present. I contend that this historical dynamism can be identified and dramatised aesthetically in ways that activate clues found in archives, artefacts, landscapes, middens and collections; clues that are primed in some way for an imaginatively *forensic* treatment.

Preface

We can define 'forensic' these ways: 'brought into the forum'; 'roused from some hidden status into explicit activity'; and 'causing a shy detail to come alive and carry an argument or generate a conviction in the public domain'. Thus forensic activity is inseparable from remembrance because to remember is first to detect some lurking charge in a skerrick or a trace, and next to channel that latency so that it is a surge that zings some vivacity (at best) or some aggravation (in less felicitous circumstances) over to at least one person; after which that generated 'force' can move from privacy to publicity. Explicated thus—from impending amnesia through psychological activation on the way to overt expression in the socio-political domain—an isolated or 'occult' phenomenon might become communal as it is remembered. It might get retrieved from encroaching oblivion prior to being rendered extensive and resilient in shared consciousness so long as the present continues to burgeon from each disintegrating last instant.

Which means that there is necessarily a personal experience inherent to every sequence of remembrance. So the prose in this book often has a testimonial tone and a first-person voice, as I try to account for what goes on (first in myself and then in the larger world) when mnemonic forces are focused and channelled through the things I regard as memoryscopes.

I hope this first-person approach brings immediacy rather than mere self-indulgence to the ideas that are put to work and subjected to scrutiny in most of the chapters. And I hope it becomes obvious that personal involvement in experiences and with artefacts is essential to grasping the definitive qualities of the processes of remembrance.

Deploying the testimonial voice and the personal focus throughout this book, therefore, I have developed a set of propositions about some interconnected themes—remnants, forensics, aesthetics—that should help us think more incisively about the closely felt momentum that is always mashing the past, present and future in contemporary life.

With the help of some select memoryscopes we might begin to see better what the Stoics are supposed to have seen all too well: that 'everything exists in the present, even the past'.[1] More on this presently.

Notes
1   Bernard Cache, *Earth Moves: the furnishing of territories*, MIT Press, 1995, p.22.

1

THE FLOOD OF ASSOCIATIONS

This essay is set at the southern end of Australia. It is concerned with how one's self, one's society and a habitat of well-tended places that are steeped in historical time can all be connected via mnemonic artefacts and practices. With this account, I want to understand how tracts of country and drafts of consciousness can mingle and fashion each other in long processes of remembrance when each beat of the present lays down the past over lifetimes, across generations, throughout ecologies and geographies, and inside societies, all knitted by actively remembering individual psyches.

So my writing needs a personal tone. For critical distance—maintained with third-person diction and disembodied cerebration—would miss many of the closely felt pulses of remembrance that I want to anatomise and survey here. In other words I want to manage the tone of the prose so that I can give you, the reader and rememberer, the option of considering, as you read, your own inseparability from the experience of remembrance. Because remembrance happens *to* you and *in* you—often spurred, admittedly, by whatever mnemonic prompts you might encounter at the edges of yourself—I would be distorting the experience, the *event* of remembrance, if I contrived to keep myself and yourself at a distance from the phenomena being investigated in the discourse.

This account puts you and me in the process, therefore. Asking you to project, imagine and remember, my essay starts with you in a car, heading out of the colonial capital of the Australian state of Victoria.

After you have driven three hours from Melbourne into the pastoral tracts of the Western District, you cross an exposed flat stretch leading to the town of Camperdown. At the verge of this hamlet, a hillock gives the road a gentle climb, and then you ease over a shallow crest, down to where slow-speed signs mark the civic boundaries.

Camperdown is snug in a lull of land that is not quite a hollow. Tidy houses and shops cluster around municipal buildings that are built staunch in the local bluestone. Protected from the tough westerly winds because the streets are cupped all around by modest rises, it is cosier here than on the plain you have just crossed. Everything feels still and settled in Camperdown. Then as you travel northwesterly out the other side of the town, you meet the next undulating crest when you bank left in an arc around the volcanic crater-rim of neighbouring Lake Gnotuk.

At this moment you comprehend how the hills puckering all around are part of some larger warp-and-weft that is patterned into the country. You recall how the car has been lolling across the countryside for the last hour or so—rising, falling, rising, every five hundred metres—like a boat cruising on the waves of a placid ocean. There is a reason this tract of land is known as The Stony Rises.

In fact Camperdown nestles between a couple of terrestrial wave-peaks that were made by surface agitation during the volcanic times when all this plain was a smear of lava popping magma bubbles that formed ringed ridges and craters that became lakes once the earth had firmed. At the outskirts of the town, you can climb one of these ridges to see how the road you have driven along is a *record*.[1] The road traces through a vast physical record of volcanic actions. Arrayed at geographical scale, the road threads through country that is a materialised memory of hot fluid cooling and solidifying. The country undulates in contact with deep time. Remembering deep time. The past is right there, laid out in the ground. When you envisage the lava oozing, you can see how the country holds its original fluidity still in its topography today.

Fluidity defines this country. The surface of the land undulates; the weather up above pulsates, minute by minute, bringing bluster with the wind and rain; wild, slow-throbbing light flares and bastes bruised clouds tumbling massive above the crater lakes; the temperature rises and falls in a breathing rhythm, as does the humidity; and before long, with a slower diurnal beat that draws night-time in, starlight shimmers in an obsidian vault.

Remembering with eels and water

Then there is the annual arrival of the eels. This is a pulse that is both naturally driven and culturally governed. Across the coastal floodplains at the back-end of the Western District out toward Warrnambool, throngs of eels travel in a breeding cycle that distributes them in prodigious migratory arcs through salt and fresh water from spawning grounds off New Guinea, down past the Barrier Reef and the Eastern Australia seaboard to the chilly southern ocean, into the Victorian river systems, and then out and north again, three thousand kilometres contrary to the current, back to the tropical Coral Sea.

Many generations ago, in the basalt lowlands at this coastal edge of the Western District, the indigenous people studied the upwelling and the draining of the seasonal waters until they learned how to improve the existing landscape by constructing ramparts of stacked stone that combine artfully with water-scoured run-off channels. Across centuries of arduous, unglamorous labour, the people of the eel country fashioned and maintained immense networks of cairned dams that guide the divagating fish across the Lake Condah floodplain. Stone upon stone, the people worked on the country and worked it into themselves thereby, making for themselves an inter-generational identity stitched to this place that they tended so assiduously. With each countless placement and replacement of stone, iteration after iteration, season after season, they made an abiding memory with the basaltic matter. Culture and nature produced together a legacy for the unborn, a communal continuity made with labour and harvest and ceremonies of perennial return.

The eels move through this watery world in teeming numbers, particularly in the rainy season when the remnant-lakes swell and the volcanic plain fills like a colander in a tub. Then as this weather cycle turns and the waters subside, stacked-stone traps herd the oily fish into covert collection bays that have been designed to expose the writhing food when the ebb-flows of water pulse away to the coast. Nearby these corrals, you can still visit, touch and *smell* enormous hollowed trees, centuries old, where the eels were hung, smoked, dried and stored as sustenance for the coming year.

Imagining the eel harvest and all the songs and stories and ceremonies associated with it, you might begin to understand a cycle of rhythmic replenishment that has become characteristic of the Western District, and you might get an inkling of how the natural world can give shape to the cultural world when the inhabitants and the environment collaborate to sustain continuous vitality in a place over time. This unstinting rhythm of work ensures that the future keeps unfurling through the present out of the past. It is a process that is as historical as it is natural, and it involves memorial practices therefore: practices of statement and reiteration, of fabrication, performance and repetition designed to charge places and times with urgency as well as with semantically communicable meanings. Over time, by dint of survival, the land and its pulses, its morphology and its people all have been made to comprise a system that garners cross-generational longevity for every vital being that is productively integrated to this portion of the world, no matter how narrowly or broadly we define 'being' and 'vitality'.

For the Western District has stayed coherent. Despite the recent depredations of colonialism, the District continues to grow out of the past. Organisation trumps disintegration. Vitality thrums and rules over morbidity. There is something 'undead' and relentless—cultural as much as natural—in the place, something that will not be easily stanched.

I borrow this notion of 'undeadness' from Eric Santner who, with his enigmatic meditation on the 'creaturely' force that he detects in his encompassing world of post–World War II Europe, seeks a kind of spiritual understanding of home that is also pragmatic, historical, ecological and psychological. For Santner, a 'creaturely' force courses through any worldly system that has not succumbed to inertness, that has been kept *significant* through cultural determination. This force 'constrains' and 'excites' everything in the lively configurations of culture, granting all elements therein access to the welling 'dimension of surplus animation' that Santner calls 'undeadness'.[2]

This 'surplus animation' is an active kind of worldly memory, something made by people and installed in places and times so that retrieval can be activated by wilful, recalling subjects. The surplus animation is well exemplified in the eel country, in the material constructs of the stone traps, in the ritualised practices of hunting and cooking, and in ceremonies and narratives that have been performed annually across many centuries and that the descendants of the eel people still share now in adapted reiterations. This is to say that the eel-memories are more than vestigial, even in the aftermath of colonialism and ecological calamity. This surplus animation in the country and in all its interdependent beings is a practical, deliberately husbanded activeness, a continuously restorative process of willed remembering, not some mystical animus.

Understood as a process of applied encryption and exegesis that stays active so long as the present is uttered out of the past, the notion of 'surplus animation' resonates with Robert Pogue Harrison's contention that 'nature and culture have at least this much in common: both compel the living to serve the interests of the unborn'.[3] Which means that everything undead is indebted to the dead so long as remembrance can pay the value of the dead forward in the currency of communicable knowledge that has already been harvested by past sojourners, so long as 'the dead, through the care of the living, perpetuate their afterlives and promote the interests of the unborn'.[4] So the stones in the eel traps are not dead things. In fact they are more like beings. They prevail from the past and bring nourishment and a sense of momentum to the cusp of the future.

From the particular qualities of the eel country, we might extrapolate some general principles for defining some prompts, processes and products of remembrance that can get performed over generational time on a societal scale. It is with continuous, custodial work—memory-work—that undeadness prevails and the interests of the unborn are served. This work lives as something memorial lodged in human bodies; but also in places, in landscapes, in other organic presences in the earth; in minerals too; and in physical forces such as wind patterns, seasonal cycles, tides and moon phases. All this potential for storage and retrieval of information and knowledge is effectively a massed memory working together. It is a system of enchantment that is maintained by highly trained technicians who are always finessing the immense memorial technology that they have made from the country.

If you baulk at calling the country itself *memory*, I would remind you that this landscape is subject to persistent, integrative forces that never stop carrying an organised, biotic rhythm from life through death and back over to the next generation being born in the eco-system of the lava-plains. And human work—*human memory-work* in the maintenance of the eel traps and smoking trees, in the songs, dances, tales and fishing-trips—ensures that a combined human and organic memory continues to serve as an integrative force that is always replenishing against depletion while pulsing laboriously and productively through the Western District. The country grows out of the remembered past. Vitality rules over morbidity. Undeadness presses through systematic memory to involve animal, vegetable and mineral components in the pulses of the landscape. Moreover, human beings are just one set of animals, merely one of the myriad elements remembering here. Indeed, if you were to insist on a hierarchical account of all life here, then the eels would have to be sovereign. And close behind would be the millions of stacked stones comprising not only the eel traps and dams and herding channels but also the dry-stone walls that mark out the farmlands over hundreds of kilometres. But really, every memory-soaked element in this lively landscape is best understood as an equal (but different) systematic component cohering in a larger, headless kind of remembering-body that is best known with the Aboriginal–English word 'country'.

The arrival of Europeans in the Western District two centuries ago damaged the indigenous societies that have been in and of this country for ten to fifteen thousand years, at least, since the cessation of the most recent volcanic activity. There would have been, and may still be, ancient stories accounting for the oozy topographics of this place. Colonialism has assailed the narratively stored and transmitted systems that have long processed the information and the remembered experiences that hold the lore for these primary societies. Much knowledge has been broken and gone missing or quiet since the influx of the Europeans. So this old knowledge is mostly dismembered now and can be remembered mainly with bold speculation. But some knowledge is still held close, stored in strategic silence, extant among the careful survivors but not shared with the interlopers.

This brings us to the crucial notion, the reason I have tarried so long in describing the pulsed character of the Western District: for the indigenous and the incursive societies both, the land itself is a memory system not unlike the Classical mnemonic palaces that Frances Yates once described, but with organic undulations added.[5] For indigenous and incursive cultures, albeit in different registers and across different arcs of time, memories are stored all over the country, ready to be recalled in and about particular places when the pertinent seasonal moments and ceremonial conditions dictate.

And the stories that are told—by indigenous or incursive narrators, no matter which—are accounts of *fluidity*. The country dictates that fluidity is the essence of all existence here. Therefore all that is known and all that is remembered is in fluid form, including the landscape itself. Memory is unthinkable here except as a system of pulses, an endlessly sluicing rhythm of depletion and repletion. The country holds memories of fluidity. But more than that, the country shows how memory *is* fluidity. The country is a tangible, inhabitable example of how memory works in individuals and communities. This is not to say the country is just a metaphor for memory. Rather, the country here *is* memory. It is a materially exact manifestation of how memory works to make the sensible world at the same time as the world whelps and hosts all its memorial entities—animal, vegetable, mineral. Memory organises and animates all the undead elements that carry patterns of purposeful action and reactions and meanings and affections across all their generations, out of the past into the future.

Memory, country, body, mind

The Australian environment is strewn with the debris of systems that were once functional and robust. These include: indigenous systems of hunting and fire-farming; narrative systems that allow the storage and recovery of lore; and endemic ecological systems as well as some ancient procedures of land-husbandry that have been recently imported, such as peasant customs of agrarian place-making; plus the metropolitan urbanism of modern European and American cultures. Especially since the Europeans arrived, much has been forgotten here. Which means there is much to imagine that must supplement the portions remaining as traces in the landscape, remaining as recall-triggers in the spatial, organic and social memory of the place.

This imagining serves the 'surplus animation' that Santner lauds, and it is partly fictive speculation and partly historic remembrance. 'Remembrance' is a *bodily* word drawn from two roots—'*memor*': to be mindful; and '*membrum*': a limb. When you remember, you put a body back together by coordinating some disaggregated, wasted or severed members. You re-member a dis-membered thing. You organise thoughts and feelings. With remembrance you become mindful in the present by bringing component parts of some past body of experience or significance back together in your sense-supplied cognition. And having remembered, you ask yourself, does this thing hold firm now? Is it plausible? Does it flex with the shapes and shifts of my experience? Does it make integrated sense when recalled to the present? Does it feel lively and entire?

Remembrance can help portions of the world persist undead. For example, it helps an inhabited landscape stay known as a live thing, sensible as an integrated body that is always pulsing, spending and replenishing. The accrued meaning of this part of the world is kept true, as past impressions are matched and proved against present perceptions.

More than just a holding bay, though, remembrance can *bring back* the gone world. In many cultures, memorial ceremonies and performances are often charged with blooming joy rather than steeped in anxious vigilance shored against the leaching that worries with amnesia.

Such a push of thrilling replenishment galvanises many indigenous Australian cultures. For example, David Mowaljarlai, the great lore-man and philosopher from Kimberley country in northern Australia, used to speak of a guiding force or energy that would 'swing' through and around him when he needed orientation in his home country.[6] My guess is he was describing a precise form of mindfulness that was informed by his homeland, the place where he learned and taught so much memory-work throughout

The Flood of Associations

his long life. Certainly he was describing remembrance as a joyous, infusing repletion, not an anxious stanch against depletion.

There is a vivacious pulse in Mowaljarlai's language when he describes being in country, being washed in a flood of associations, drenched in an upwelling of memories and stored portions of knowledge distributed throughout the country. Notably, the Kimberley is water-pulse country. In this respect (if in almost no other) it is similar to the Victorian Western District. Each place is soaked in its peculiar animus of replenishment. Each stretch of country—walked, worked, sung and parsed by its knowledgeable custodians—shows how remembered coherence can surge in a joyous influx. In healthy memory-country, the dismembered mnemonic fragments are poised for the guidance of the celebrating exegete. Depletion can be washed with repletion when recalled fragments integrate to bring the full body of a felt record quickly burgeoning in response to mnemonic triggers that are arrayed across the landscape.

In the poet Robert Gray's Australian variations on aphoristic format, he observes that:

> The world, it seems, is the maximum
> Number of things, or of forces,
> That can exist together.[7]

Which shows me how to conclude my brief account of landscape mnemonics here…by mis-remembering, translating and expanding Gray's canny axiom:

> In service of the pulsating world, memory, it seems,
> Is the most forceful
> Minimum of stored and charged details

That can be made to flow restoratively into each other
Over time.

Notes
1 The importance and etymology of the word 'record' will be examined in chapter three of this book.
2 E. Santner, *On Creaturely Life: Rilke, Benjamin, Sebald*, The University of Chicago Press, Chicago, 2006, p. 105.
3 R. P. Harrison, *The Dominion of the Dead*, The University of Chicago Press, Chicago, 2003, p. ix.
4 Harrison, p. 40.
5 See F. Yates, *The Art of Memory*, Penguin, Harmondsworth, 1969. See also J. Spence, *The Memory palace of Matteo Ricci*, Faber, London, 1985.
6 Consult D. Mowaljarlai, ABC Radio National 'Law Report', 1995: <http://www.abc.net.au/rn/talks/8.30/lawrpt/lstories/lr311001.htm> This interview is also quoted in S. Muecke, *Ancient and Modern: time, culture and indigenous philosophy*, UNSW Press, Sydney, 2004, p. 172. See also J. Malnic and D. Mowaljarlai, *Yorro Yorro: everything standing up alive*, Magabala Books, Broome, 1993.
7 R. Gray, 'Epigrams' in *New Selected Poems*, 2nd edition, Duffy & Snellgrove, Sydney, 1998, p. 296.

2

PLACES PAST DISAPPEARANCE

For thirty years now, I have been publishing in a variety of media, usually starting out by responding to some peculiar cache of shards or remnants, each cache broken by time or wilful neglect, barely prevailing over disarray. Slowly I have come to realise that the absences, *the negative spaces*, always prompt the work.

For example, with a team of collaborators I have spent several years responding to a pictorial archive, a great collection of mysterious scenes gathered in Sydney throughout most of the twentieth century. In a suite of artworks known collectively as *Life After Wartime*, viewers are encouraged to figure how to account for a salvaged batch of crime-scene photographs that no longer have any official, conclusive documents attached to them.[1]

Another example of this kind of 'vestige work' is my book *Seven Versions of an Australian Badland*, which is a literary meditation on a fraught and fragmented tract of failed profiteer scrub in tropical Queensland.[2]

Always, with this vestige work, I encounter the following kinds of questions:

> What has gone missing here?
> How can we imagine functional coherence here?
> What if these dumb portions of culture could get some eloquence and talk to each other?

Normally I would not expect anyone to care much about my arcane fascinations. Except, I see hundreds of other Australian artists and writers working in the same way, examining aftermaths and discontinuities, trying to re-build systematic comprehension in response to fragments. And while I cannot speak for so many others, I have a hunch that it might be useful to try to understand, in public, what it means when one gets so *attached* to untethered things. Why this society-wide compulsion to know the negative spaces?

So here is my account of the chase after this hunch.

Rummaging in Australia's aftermath cultures, I look to redress the disintegration in our story-systems, in our traditional knowledge caches, our landscapes and ecologies. The job is to investigate and recuperate scenes and collections of artefacts that have been torn apart somehow: torn by landgrabbing, let's say, or by accidents, or by exploitation that ignores rituals of preservation and restoration. Typically, the scenes and systems that get investigated were once more cohesive, but now they are ailing or out of balance. I have come to understand that most of Australia is like this: that the place I inhabit carries so much raggedness in it because it is patterned, day in, day out, by a society that has used its environment more roughly than carefully.

The situation is not entirely bleak, however. Even in the aftermath of neglect or abuse, systems usually retain tendencies and traces from their previous cogency. These traces offer chances for re-formatting, even though it is pointless to dream of retrieving and settling back into some pristine, pre-lapsarian world.

The job is reanimation. It is a reiterative application of meanings to places over time. Or, to borrow Morris Berman's terminology, such work is the secular 're-enchantment of the world'.[3] It is an attempt to chant some patterned significance and cogency back into places that have long been denied custodial care. It is the first step in imagining how a new, relatively cohesive present might evolve from the adjustment and activation of vestiges from the past.

The Australian part of the world is strewn with remnants of cultural and natural systems. Consider the vulnerable skeins of Indigenous dreaming; consider the residues of endemic ecologies; consider the myriad systems of work and belief that have been refined elsewhere in the world and only partially transplanted here away from their original contexts. The good news is that in some cases, despite two hundred years of colonial disturbance, terminal damage has been avoided, either by getting out of the way of resurgent nature or by applying design and labour attentively and adaptively. But in many instances our places are teetering with a minimal degree of systematic cohesion, and they will be made sensible only if we act promptly and boldly, so that our aesthetic and civic patterns might help us project our thinking across everything that is missing or ailing. In other words, we need to imagine across all the absence.

Our parlous states need to be recuperated imaginatively. We need to propose 'what if' scenarios that help us account for what has happened in our habitat so that we can then better envisage what *might* happen in an improved situation. We need to apprehend the past, to assay the historical momentum that is abroad in the world. We need to divine and perhaps redirect the continuous tendencies that are constructing us as they emerge from the past to make the present. (I will return to this tendentious term 'divination' before too long.) By synchronising ourselves to the inherent, historically configured tendencies that flow through a place in time, we stand a chance of avoiding exhaustion as we try to change the current state of things, as we try to understand how to alter the world and ourselves.

To reiterate: our parlous states need imagination. I define imagination as:

- an ability to venture in one's mind out past a comfortable, known limit;
- an ability to discern feasible relationships where they are not obvious, to see how portions, clues or details might be put into relationships that generate forceful meanings or pulses of feeling;
- a readiness to incorporate the unknown, embodied in psychological or aesthetic form, so that we might be emboldened to alter, so that we might let ourselves into otherness and vice versa.

Imagination is needed when one encounters evidence that is in smithereens. I try to keep this in mind when confronted with the disheveled scenes and archives and collections that are so representative of contemporary Australia, when confronted with so many systems that have vestiges of coherence but are not entire, not conclusive or composed. I try to remember not only that these are systems where imagination is needed, but also that imagination can be strengthened here and that these systems offer opportunities for self-alteration.

A specific example? *Seven Versions of an Australian Badland*, researched and written throughout the 1980s and 1990s, is a book that examines a district where colonial landgrabbing and monocultural farming have plundered the environment to the extent that it now appears like a defiled and exhausted thing. Across five decades—given that I have visited and re-visited the place since I was a child—I have traversed this broken country countless times, with a growing conviction that it is a disintegrated scree of evidence that bears witness to the conflicting historical forces that have built it and continue to shape it.

In *Seven Versions*, I call this territory 'a vast, historical crime scene'. In such landscapes—and they are everywhere in Australia—we have to ask ourselves, what can be made of this place now? What can we know about its piecemeal ecology, its choppy geomorphics and scarified townscapes? How can we overhear the pertinent gossip—the attempts at truth and the self-serving lies—that buzz about it? What of the journey-patterns, the shuttling rhythms stitching the place together in time, now and in the past? What can we make of the documents that have been generated in response to this country? And what of the absences—when are they meaningful, when are they nothing?

In the Central Queensland hinterland, my historically informed imagination produced a book in which I tried to make manifest some forces that are usually only *latent* within this somewhat systematic and somewhat disintegrated tract of country. In the case of another work—a suite of museum exhibits and multimedia installations entitled *Life After Wartime*, most of which were made in collaboration with Kate Richards—the imaginative response is a story-system that proffers restless, plausible patterns of speculation regarding the enigmatic scenes in an archive of forensic photography. In each case we arrive at the evidence in the aftermath of some deep stun and metamorphosis—an ecosystem has collapsed, a man has died in his car outside a trade union office, for example—and we try to account for how the scene has ended up like this. What got us from then and there to here and now? We try to insert some persuasive notions—be they thoughts, theories or emotions—throughout the partial array of evidence, to show how even these riddled things can get better integrated, to show how they might help us know more fully the forces and flows that made the world they came from and make the world they have stopped in. (By the way, we will return to *Life After Wartime* several times throughout this book, inspecting it from different angles, with different thematic lenses.)

When deploying 'supplementary imagination' like this, the crucial factor is the *restlessness*, the way the artwork that you produce—be it a book, a database, a building, a park or a garden—prompts the perceiver's speculation by artful imbalances and implied possibilities for completion or patterning. The supreme example of the aesthetic of generative incompleteness might be found in Zen temples and gardens, where the visitor experiences an environment that is 'charged' with a powerful 'urge': a flowing potentiality that is more implied than shown. Norman Carver expresses it pithily. In Zen architecture, he explains, load-bearing elements often establish a 'heavy structural beat' (in roof beams and wall posts, for example) which is counterpointed delicately by textures, surfaces and apertures (in paper screens, pebbled concrete and tatami patterns, for example) which infuse the scene with a 'rhythmic complexity' that relieves or interweaves with the beat.[4] Thus the urge for supplementation dwells as much in the perceiving visitor as in the environment. The carefully set-up incompletion in the artwork—verging on ineffability—drives a generative aesthetic that makes every encounter with the Zen work a continuous event that occurs in internal (or psychic) space as well as in external (or physical) space. After a while in such environments, visitors often feel an urge to imagine some large pattern cohering *everywhere*, even though such a pattern is not explicitly present in the artfully 'unresolved' space that the visitors are inhabiting. If you spend a full day in one temple you undergo, literally, a mind-altering exercise. And the urge for pattern-completion often helps you feel inseparable from the extensive environment, attuned to some flowing integrity in it. (There is some Shinto pantheism and animism in this sensation, no doubt.) As Carver proclaims, to round out his argument: in Zen architecture, 'all relationships are abbreviated and subtle, encouraging the exercise of the imagination in grasping the whole'.[5]

The literary side of Zen is instructive too. What you get from a haiku, for example, is a compulsion to imagine beyond the detail, to get an inkling in the poem's intense fragment so that you can envisage a larger world related to that intensified portion, a larger world of interconnections made instantaneously and intuitively comprehensible by the tiny shock that a good haiku produces. As Thomas Hoover has explained so well, 'the mind is struck as with a hammer, bringing the senses up short and releasing a flood of associations'.[6]

Floods, flows, urges, surges, continuities: such words bring us close to what I seek when exercising the historically informed imagination.

I now understand such work to be a kind of divination. Take the theological connotations out of the word. And the mysticism. For me, divination is a secular activity and a technical routine whereby you can help fragments adhere and integrate so that the dis-membered elements of a scene might share some sensible connection, some re-membering. With divination, there is an urge to connect. In water divining, for example, absence bullies the system—a clear channel is missing between the water and the quester. The diviner has to ponder the possible links between the self and the water, thus filling in the missing conduits of a severed circuitry and vaulting over the absences to form cogency where once there was dishevelment. In this way the diviner is a kind of 'ammeter', measuring potentiality or energy, tracking its flows and blockages and engineering ways to marshal the current back to connectivity. It is the way much Indigenous traveling proceeds—figuring when and where to move according to a sense of the most amenable flow of connections in the place at the time. And it is very like the energy-sensing described by the old Indigenous law-man David Mowaljarlai (as mentioned in the previous chapter) when he used to talk of the guiding forces that 'swing' through him in his Kimberley country.[7] Also it resembles the responsive wayfinding detailed by Will Kyselka in his visionary study of Polynesian navigation, *An Ocean in Mind*.[8]

I am sure these are all processes requiring intuition. Intuition is a faculty that can be learned and refined. Sportspeople know this. They devote a large proportion of their training to the development of intuition. It is the same for improvising musicians and actors. When intuition ignites, sudden, holistic understanding arises. In modern parlance, it is sometimes called a 'systems view'. It is a little like trying to feel the sensations of a 'phantom limb': this awareness of something palpably present and convincing where the explicit matter is actually missing.

This term, 'phantom', is close to 'fantasy'. Which brings me to a cautionary moment. I want to emphasise that when responding to fragments of historical evidence, I am on the side of history. Without claiming to be an historian, I find myself in agreement with a great one, Greg Dening, when he said that the important historical writing occurs when scholars apply imagination to the evidence. *Imagination*, not *fantasy*, he stressed. What Dening was asserting, I think, is that one needs to retain an allegiance to the evidence. A fiction writer is not obliged to do this, making a different contract—one of imaginative *plausibility*—with the reader. However, to be historically aligned one must bear witness to particular traces that have been touched by the world and are materially available for shared inspection in the world.[9]

This leads to the centre of the issue: the conditions of living and working in the aftermath-culture of Australia are such that much of the vital evidence is either missing, immaterial or non-textual. And the evidence that we do have is often partial, broken or sometimes obscured in denials. Which means that conventional historiographical protocols come up short when we try to get the fullest possible comprehension of the past that has whelped our present. In Australia we need to imagine across gaps and quandaries in the evidence; we need to venture out past what is known, what is familiar, what is authorised in disciplines that were founded elsewhere.

I trust it is clear that I am not declaring conventional history to be insular or useless. I am saying it is only partially useful. Just as imaginative speculation is only partially useful. Together, though, they might be productive, if we found ways to loosen and interlace the borders around historiography and speculation, if we found ways to narrate across everything that is missing in our modes of envisaging and understanding.

In a radio interview about *Seven Versions*, a journalist asked me: 'What is this odd book? What section of the bookstore does it go in? It doesn't have the certitude of history. So, isn't it just imaginative? Isn't it just tricky fiction?'

Responding a little absent-mindedly—a little intuitively—I had a sudden insight. 'Backfill,' I quipped, 'basically what I do is historical backfill.' Perhaps I could have said 're-enchantment', but I am glad I went the other way. As I tried to haul myself out of the sudden ditch, I realised this term 'backfill' was a useful enough idea. I explained how you can uncover fragments that you know have been discarded by the world. Real evidence. You find it lying around in jagged form and out of place, as we all do every day, and you ask yourself, 'How can I account for this material?' Quite literally, 'What are some of the accounts I might offer so that we can make provocative, connective sense with these fragments?'

So, 'backfill' happens when you offer an historically informed set of speculations:

> Maybe *this* story accounts for these bits of evidence as well as the silences that we've uncovered?
>
> How does *this account* sound as a way to explain the somewhat systematic yet somewhat broken shape of each piece of evidence?
>
> Maybe *this version* of experience can help us understand the mysterious overall form of our particular midden heap?

Backfill is what we have to enact when conventional historical techniques fail, as happens often in this place—Australia—that has been formed by so much disappearance, dissembling and dispersal. Backfill is work performed after you have done some divination, after you have attempted to intuit feasible and defensible but admittedly inconclusive accounts connecting the fragments. Backfill is necessarily an imaginative and speculative procedure. But it needs to be authoritative as well as imaginative. And I think it is the most resourceful response—opposed to silence or denial—that helps us keep on investigating when we encounter the definitive quality of post-1788 Australian history, when we encounter the fact that despite the settlers' overwhelming attention to some types of bureaucratic minutiae, many of the truly important events of our past have not made it into the textual archives. This is especially true of the cross-cultural encounters that took place on frontiers, away from the administrative offices, in situations where the traditional trace-leaving of writing often did not net what occurred.

Even so, traces did get registered by other means—in bodies, in family tale-telling, in songs, in landscapes, in sketches—and those traces do not work so well for conventional historiography. For me the supreme example is the aesthetic, transformative power of witnessing that fortifies Archie Roach's ballad, *Took the Children Away*. To hear that song is to sense a compelling proposition about the way the past—deeply felt and prevailing—has produced the present: deeply felt and prevailing. You sense great draughts of resolutely unforgotten experience in the musical patterns of the song: in the lyrics and the glissando of the voice from its palpable pain through to the exultation of survival. You sense all this and feel yourself altered by it. The song is not an anthem affirming an established creed; rather it is a three-minute transit through affective comprehension, a transit from ignorance through structured feelings that, via affect, produce a compelling effect of truth, of validity, of felt conviction. Therefore, in situations where the textual records do not net the events, other modes of accounting need to arrive after the event, to accrete around the non-textual clues.

My work in disheveled archives and in postcolonial Australia has taught me that we can perform these other types of representation productively and responsibly, conjuring propositions that are not history but are historically informed and might be sometimes more important than history because of the way they make manifest an urge to account for the disconnected fragments. Such historically informed speculations are vital because they vault over silence, denial and absence. And sometimes they change hearts and minds. These speculations draw on our capability to imagine otherness, to think past the endorsed limits, to undergo alteration. And this is crucial because if we continue to close our imaginations to the aberrations and insufficiencies in our historical records, we run the risk of slipping into an insular melancholy, fearful of the power of the interpretations we refuse to consider. It is likely we will not dwell in much joy till we get real about the darkness. For the joy will always be shadowed, and the background of gloom and denial will get heavier and more worrying because we will sense it persisting and amplifying outside of our ability to turn and face it.

But I digress a little and I sermonise. I was discussing 'backfill'. Let me conclude with a summation.

When performing historical backfill, you need to assay every testimony, every mark and song and clue available so that you can propose something compelling, something that is historically advised, persuasive and authoritative but admittedly speculative. Instead of being *conclusively* convincing, you have to cajole people into consulting their own faculties of judgment so they might match your proffered model of possibility against their received convictions. You have to encourage them to wonder, 'What do I know?', rather than to demand, 'Confirm what I believe'. You need to conjure a worldview that helps readers judge—yes, no or maybe—whether your proposition feels plausible, whether it helps them confront something true but previously occulted in their world. If you do this well, the reader is no longer a recipient of your supposed truths. Instead the reader becomes a forensic subject, an investigator and formulator of contentious systems of meaning. When an investigation is open like this, as opposed to foregone in its conclusions, then the investigator is an imaginer, someone who declines to accept common sense automatically.

Finally, to accept inconclusiveness is different from deciding that nothing compelling can be offered. The imaginative investigator keeps on speculating and testing, speculating and testing, always proposing possible worlds that are tethered to the actual world, the world of evidence despite all the abeyance. This can happen restlessly, sceptically, but with a venturesome spirit, not with desperation. The imaginative investigator works with evidence, vaults over absence and refuses silence. Such a quest, such imagination within investigation is probably our most urgent historical task right now.

Notes

1. See projects by R. Gibson and K. Richards et al., detailed at www.lifeafterwartime.com.
2. R. Gibson, *Seven Versions of an Australian Badland*, UQP, Brisbane, 2002.
3. M. Berman, *The Re-enchantment of the World*, Cornell University Press, Ithaca, 1981.
4. N. A. Carver, *Form and Space of Japanese Architecture*, Shokokusha, Tokyo, 1965, p. 65.
5. Carver, p. 156. See also N. Burch, *To the Distant Observer: form and meaning in the Japanese cinema*, Scolar Press, London, 1979, for a comprehensive explanation of how this aesthetic pervades much Japanese cinema.
6. T. Hoover, *Zen Culture*, Routledge & Kegan Paul, London, 1978 p. 205.
7. See J. Malnic and D. Mowaljarlai, *Yorro Yorro: everything standing up alive*, Magabala Books, Broome, 1993.
8. See W. Kyeselka, *An Ocean in Mind*, University of Hawai'i Press, Honolulu, 1987. This brilliant book is featured in detail in *Changescapes*, the companion-volume to *Memoryscopes*.
9. See the transcript of Greg Dening's speech to the National Library of Australia: http://www.nla.gov.au/events/history/papers/Greg_Dening.html.

3

REMEMBERING A FUTURE WITH LANDSCAPE

If you live in Australia, you are defined somewhere between two opposing myths of origin: you might tell a story of your *arising* from the country, or you might tell of your *arriving*. The most compelling versions of arising come from Indigenous people, who can refer to millennia of occupancy when claiming to be autochthonous, or 'of the earth'. By contrast, the tales of arriving are told by visitors and immigrants. Then there are the people who were born in the country but have been steeped predominantly in a culture that can be measured only in a couple of centuries rather than millennia: the people who are native-born but non-Indigenous.

For all categories of Australians, but differently in each case, one's attitude to the culturally apprehended environment or hosting landscape is crucial to how much one might claim to belong in the country. Landscape is thus a basis of personal orientation in Australia: the basis of a person's past derivations and future prospects in the local environment; the basis from which one can propose and pursue a carefully considered life in this place.

From a native-born perspective, landscape is inseparable from the idea of *place*; while at the other extreme, from an immigrant perspective, landscape must be developed from an encounter with *space*. For the purposes of this chapter, we can define place as the shared scene where occupants debate, narrate, subvert or maintain a culture that orients them in the turbulent world of fate, nature, history and political power. Place is a custodial phenomenon involving practices in time as well as topography, while space is a neutral entity awaiting actions that bring significance. Space can become territory or property if appropriated in particular ways. Or it can become place if incorporated more assiduously and ritually into systems that give rise to personal or communal awareness. Enacted along a spectrum stretching between place and space, the making and maintaining of landscapes is a practice that folds the country in and out of its occupants. With landscapes, you can assay the extent to which you feel well placed, the extent to which you believe that you come *from* rather than *to* the land. You can test whether you know a place in your bones or whether you know it to be 'over there', framed and separate from yourself. With landscapes, you can see people making a place for themselves.

Placemaking in Australia is a process of recovering and sometimes inventing rituals that help people tend and interpret the scenes where their lives take place. Most tracts of land in contemporary Australia used to be millennially maintained places, but then they were mistreated as profiteer spaces when the colonial incursions 'took place'.

Seized spaces usually ail because their longrunning needs are ignored or misinterpreted. Yet in the aftermath of the seizures, even with all the devolution and damage, the previous integrity of certain places can still be retrieved. Or new vivacity can be inculcated wherever custodial work begins again, in a state of repercussion and creative speculation soaked with the sad knowledge that a fully coherent version of the past country will never be retrieved now that the original systems of placement have been fractured by so many new influences pressing in.

Nowadays most landscape practice in Australia is concerned with the work of *retrieval*, whether through critiques disempowering old imperialist attitudes to space or through ritual enchantments that put careful meanings in place. Such 're-placement' usually involves ritual utterances in response to contentious scenes, to residues and to rhythms that are still stuttering in from a long time ago. This is not mysterious, nor is it mystical. Mostly it is storytelling and the enactment of ceremonies of looking, listening and moving that help people remember advice and know their options and obligations in stretches of country, to know how the environment that hosts and sustains us also needs us unless it repels us. From my non-Indigenous perspective, there seem to be similarities between such ecological ethics and many Indigenous practices of law-keeping in country. But I emphasise that I have not earned rights to profess from an Indigenous standpoint. What I have earned is the right to speak of the systems and the legacies—healthy and ailing—that people must share now across the country.

What to do with these shared places? How to practise landscape more beneficially? One must start by acknowledging that the Australian environment is strewn with the debris of systems that were once functional and robust. These include Indigenous systems of camp-making, travelling, hunting and fire-farming, narrative systems, endemic ecological systems, plus some ancient procedures of land-husbandry that have been recently imported, such as Asian, South Pacific and European-peasant customs of placemaking. In several cases, in the aftermath of so much colonial space-grabbing, contemporary Australians have managed to reverse part of the damage, either by setting scenes where resilient nature can reassert itself, or by applying well-placed analysis, technology, ceremonies and labour to rehabilitate some blighted regions. In other instances, places are teetering with a minimal degree of systematic cohesion and can be made lively only if people act promptly and radically. But it all requires *imagination*.

When applied to landscape, imagination encourages the ability to propose astute 'what if' scenarios that might help us stimulate some disrupted spaces so that the spaces can become places again. This imagining must be partly speculation and partly remembrance.

'Remember' is a word that bears examination. It is a *bodily* word, the active verb subtending the noun 'memory'. As mentioned in an earlier chapter, the word 'memory' comes from two roots—'memor': to be mindful; and 'membrum': a limb. So when you remember, you put a body back together by coordinating some disaggregated or severed members; you re-member the dis-membered entirety.

Remembering is thus an attempt to sense cohesion, cogency, and vitality in the model of the past that you are making. When you remember persuasively in a space where decay or disappearance has occurred, you are working to make that space a place. The remembrance helps with placemaking, therefore. It is part of landscape practice.

The idea of 'recording' is vital to landscape practice, particularly with regard to works of landscape art that utilise video and audio equipment. 'Record' is a startling word. It means 'to bring back to the heart'. It is from the root that makes 'cardiac', that makes 'corazon' in Spanish, 'coeur' in French, 'courage' in English. To move something once again through the heart: this is what you do when you record something. The well-retrieved record becomes part of the personal and cultural bloodstream, something lively and connective within a larger body of knowledge.

This leads to the idea that you might know something not only in the bones but in the blood. Such a state of knowing *entirely*, such a state of embodied, holistic knowledge: it is worth yearning for, worth working for. You can find lifeblood in country. The well-recorded landscape can become part of a body politic therefore. And the well-recorded landscape can be known as a body *aesthetic* too, when the country has been rendered keenly perceptible by all the senses. You can be incorporated and involved in well-recorded country. Sustenance and maintenance bolster each other there.

Somewhat aesthetical, somewhat ecological, this mode of knowing a place is difficult to describe technically, but when you work with recorded country and especially with remembrance in landscapes, you sometimes get a sense that the coherence of the place is holding together partly because the landscape is prompting for you (and in you) some insights that you already know and partly because the place is goading your intuition with an indistinct hint or detail that connects you to some larger cohesion that was once abroad in the past of a place and that you are now working to know better. This feeling 'in the blood', this intuition about a larger cohesion, comes in a moment when the integrated knowledge of a place starts emerging. You get a pulse of conviction conjoining yourself to the larger world of well-placed, historical experience. From this systematic feeling, you get a chance to imagine, to offer compelling 'what if' scenarios built on the fragments and absences that you are now remembering as a coherent, vital model of the world that you are heir to.

Such involvement in place gets recorded again and again in contemporary landscape practices in Australia. So much more than decorative or descriptive, contemporary Australian landscape has to be construed as ontological, political and moral as well as imaginative and workaday. Engaging with a landscape in Australia, contending with all the elements that do and do not connect up, you have to project some *integrity* into the array of clues. This integrative work is also *expansive* insofar as it stretches at your definitions of the self even as it is generated by your own subjectivity, and it casts you into doubt all the time because the elements and the absences in the scene are always replete with a great deal more than you presently know. The country has been shaped by thousands of human generations, after all.

In historically informed work, the past has forgotten more than you will ever know. Or to say it in a more prosaic way, what you already know is useful but it is never adequate or conclusive. Therefore when you encounter landscapes in Australia, you have to remind yourself to go through imaginative processes that change your self as you try to think up some good 'what if' propositions in response to the skerricks that the past has left behind in response to what you don't know for sure.

Which brings us to the all-important phenomenon of *alteration*. It's a notion full of changefulness implying a continuous new start, and paradoxically I'd like to conclude this present meditation with this notion of alteration, because the placemaking issues we've been addressing need to be endless.

To undergo alteration is to find oneself becoming other than what one was a moment ago. Alteration can entail speculative expansion. When a place challenges you not only to remember but also to speculate across its absences even as you are informed by your received knowledge, then you are undergoing alteration. You alter a landscape by offering interpretations about it, but you also undergo an alteration in your self because you encounter the qualms and quandaries that the scene presents. And when sensing the need for a more comprehensive integration between yourself and your place, you are usually forced to try out new propositions that might proffer a new sense of integrity in the scene. Incorporating the most persuasive of these propositions, you become slightly 'otherwise'. You become the country this way, even as the country becomes you. Such self-extension, such alteration and enfolding of self and place is the way much contemporary landscape is heading in Australia.

The situation is urgent. The millions of Australians who are not trained custodians of the environment have perhaps one last chance to become otherwise, to know their place by earning the right to receive some permissible portions of old, well-placed knowledge. After earning such learning, and being emboldened also to be imaginative with the speculative scenarios that we all must now invent and chant into our scenes, we might conjure new models for knowing our place in this grievously altered old environment where we are all fated now to survive or perish. Such is the work of the landscape artist in Australia: to draw on the past and sketch out a future. And in its endlessness, the work of the landscaper, the place-recorder and rememberer entails a great deal more than just framing and perspective.

4

'ALL THINGS ARE IN CONTACT'
—ARCHIVES, MEMORY, IMAGINATION

I visit Kyoto regularly. Many years ago, preparing for my first sojourn there, I asked an experienced visitor what I should do on day one. She advised I bus out to the temple precinct at Daitoku-ji and spend the afternoon mooching among the Rinzai sect gardens. She quipped, 'It's like speed-Zen'.

Decades later, I think this advice was canny. More wise than wry, my friend gave me the means to get started. Like a kōan, her counsel was ironic and sincere, senseless and sensible. For all its insufficiency and vapidity, the speed-Zen approach has merit because it gives you an ordinary way into the mysteries. Ignoring mandatory first portals into the Zen sensibility, you are freed from the surfeit of reverence and significance that usually overwhelms a newcomer to Kyoto. With speed-Zen—despite how wrong it is in its swiftness and cognitive grabbiness—you do stand a chance of being shocked and stimulated by odd conjunctions. You might see, for example, how a revered garden path can be crash-edited against a glimpse of a tiny child crouching to inspect a stand of moss while her huge robot-shaped backpack peers companionably over her shoulder and absorbs the full world with unblinking serenity; or you might savour the vision of a monk polishing the hubcaps of his tangerine Mitsubishi while on the other side of the compound wall an advertising van chimes out a rendition of *Jingle Bells* generated from a digital synthesiser's version of Caribbean steel drums. After all, it is from these quotidian montages that epiphanies sometimes spark. And through these tiny fissures in commonsense, so long as you can believe that a logic other than chance or chaos subtends them, you might eventually register some gleams of new understanding about the forces that jostle people and nature in space throughout time.

I tell this little parable because it is much the same with archives. Now that the world is overladen with its own records, there is a smothering legacy to comprehend. Too much access and authority and importance are pressed upon ponderous vaults of heritage. Which makes a welter of daunting questions:

- If you are trying to know something about all this batched information, how can you get started?
- What is the right way in?
- How can you get any systematic new understanding from the massed records?
- By what means will you grasp some knowledge that is unaccustomed, startling and worth shifting your commonsense to accommodate?
- From traces remembering the past, how do you get fresh insights into the present and how might you conjure new possibilities for the coming world?

Archives are defined both by their content and by their indexing, which is really a kind of logic for storing and finding each piece of content. Furthermore, the great archives (with their content and their indexing) are like the temple gardens (with their plants and their landscapes). Both are arranged and maintained to prompt revelation from the synthesis of the component parts. With this third capacity—the prompting of revelation—several details combine to become more than mere sums. But first, before any associative surprises can spring from the amalgamated traces, you need an index or way in to all the stored details.

As Daitoku-ji is to Zen, so Charles Merewether's book *The Archive: documents of contemporary art* is to cultural history. With this lean and filleted miscellany, you can go mooching among an optimal minimum of the key texts, speed-learning some fundamental tenets both of information management and of citational aesthetics. In Merewether's collection you will get (i) a critical mass of content—just enough—and (ii) some indexing that clusters texts in chapter-categories named 'Inscriptions', 'Traces', 'Contestations' and 'Retracings'. With a deliberate irreverence, the categories bristle against each other, provoking and disturbing rather than settling on a singular view or polemic. Which is no more or less than is promised. For the book is just a way in, a means to start thinking and talking about archival intelligence.

The inscriptions and the traces are excerpts from Sigmund Freud, Walter Benjamin, Giorgio Agamben, Jacques Derrida, Allan Sekula, Paul Ricoeur and Michel Foucault. All of these authorities are queued up to stock the collection with truncated treatises concerning ontology, memory, materiality, clues and signs. Then the curators and artists get to contest and retrace. Again and again, with a boisterous range of methods and tones, the artists show how any archive is a modelled world deserving and repaying interrogation, wonder, suspicion and all of the other attitudes applicable to the actual world. Christian Boltanski, Marcel Broodthaers, Eugenio Dittborn and the Atlas Group represent their caste with enigma and élan. Also, the sprit of Dada and the Surrealists is strong everywhere in the artists' testimonies, with their repeated refusals to bend into the shapes of governance and with their cultish appreciation of the unexpected conjunction.

But it is the figure of the curator that emerges as the revelation. Merewether (a curator himself) is there in the body of the text, as are Benjamin Buchloh and Okwui Enwezor, each of them demonstrating how much the way in matters most when you are encountering a huge payload of the past's stored meaning and emotion. Of course, the curator is paid to make these indexes and orientations, and there is an art to curation nowadays—something intuitively quick and complex—precisely because the world is stuffed now with so many records, so much legacy: such an amnesiating profusion of memory to be marshalled.

In Merewether's compendium, the Delhi-based Raqs Media Collective (www.raqsmediacollective.net) stand out as exemplary. A loose but rule-governed gathering of collaborators and researchers, Raqs are greater than the sum of their individual members. They work in, with and as communities, often running education programs at the same time as they interpret scenes, provoke scenarios and purvey interpretations. And with everything they do and cause, they record and store the results online, in books, on charts, throughout the international circuits of conferences and art biennales. Equally artists, archivists, curators and bureaucrats, Raqs use information as their matter. Or, more precisely, they use the potential for relationships associated with information. They show how stored information can be a medium (or a way through) leading to communitarian cognition and affection.

This idea of the power in relationships (not only amongst people but also amongst echelons of data and desires and organisational tendencies) is the great notion that has spread from cybernetics through many disciplines in humanities and social sciences. In the art world, the notion has been made famous and somewhat too ubiquitous by Nicolas Bourriaud's books *Relational*

'All Things are in Contact'

Aesthetics and *Postproduction*.[1] Concerning practices of archiving, the relational idea gives special force to the latest definitions of indexing and synthesis. Using the index to search glosses on initial ideas or hunches, an investigator can work toward the synthesis of a new understanding by pulling these glosses into agglomerations, watching for the coherence and flashes of insight generated by the relationships. In film lingo that was first extensively theorised by Sergei Eisenstein, this is the montage approach, using each chunk of information as a flint to strike against another, always hopeful for sparks. In an ever-emerging system of several struck relationships, you might get some fresh light and insight. What happens *between* the artefacts is what makes the radiance.

The montage approach rattles through Merewether's contents list. It is there in the way almost every excerpt is festooned with… ellipses…at its end or beginning. And many times, the ellipsis jigs within the body of the excerpt. Each text anthologised by Merewether trims portions from larger originals, offering a series of edited chunks that have been honed into sharpened manifestos. Each chunk is part of the larger indexical manifest that is the code governing this book-as-archive. The manifest on the contents page gives the user the chance to see what relationships might be formed by combining the available manifestos in whatever wilful way you like. Depending on how relational or how hierarchical the manifest is taken to be, all the individual elements can be more or less equalised in their availability to each other.

Merewether's book is relatively open, therefore, and it encourages the reader to flick around, back to front, hither and yon, bit by bit. But, with its introduction and its delineated beginning–middle–end retinue, it is still *a book*. It offers canonical reference points and the main stylistic and thematic guidelines. It wants to be an archive *and* it is pleased to be a book. In its hybridity it shows the limits and the possibilities of books and relational databases alike. It helps the reader begin to grasp how, at the thoroughly non-hierarchical and more dynamic end of index design, outside the bound stratigraphy of stitched-up folios, you might get something like Ralph Waldo Emerson's vision of the anti-nominalist urges that actually arrange earthly experience: 'all things are in contact', Emerson declaims in a quip that defines 'transcendentalism' more effectively than the thousands of books that have been written so far on the topic.[2]

The dyad of the manifesto versus the manifest, which gives Merewether's book its voracious 'zoom lens' quality, also brings precision and scope to Dan Adler's enthralling *Hanne Darboven: Cultural History 1880–1983*. Adler contemplates the archival theme by pulling focus tightly on an extraordinary work of archiving-as-art that was assembled by the German conceptualist Darboven between 1980 and 1983.

Adler's first task is to find or fabricate the most effective manifest for commencing the interpretation of Darboven's massive collection of texts, objects, conjunctions, fragments and befuddlements called *Cultural History 1880–1983*. Attempting an initial description of Darboven's opus, Adler declares:

> One standard approach to Cultural History is the making of a list, or manifest, of its contents...pre-WWII postcards showing city views, landscapes and tourist sites; greeting cards; pin-ups of film and rock stars; Word War I era German cigarette cards; geometric diagrams for textile weaving...animal figures, a teddy bear, a robot, a crescent moon hanging from the ceiling, a kiosk, a ceramic bust of a moustached man.[3]

The list gives a way to get started with the profligacy of the project, but it fails to catch the fecundity and the wonder in the entire midden. Deliberately, Darboven makes sure any list will fail. As Adler notes, *Cultural History 1880–1983* is 'relentlessly resistant to being read'. Confronting the work as 'an abstract whole' is provocatively and productively different from zooming one's focus in on any individual, fascinating element. The viewer is a rummager and an apprentice alchemist always oscillating between encountering momentary utterances and some mysteriously integrated system, between accumulated details and synthesised wisdom, between the manifest and the manifesto. Darboven's *Cultural History* dramatises 'the division between the personal and the universal as it operates in the process of portraying history', but she does this with alluring strangeness and arcane organisational logic, such that the full work will always 'refuse to answer the call for interpretive synthesis'. Now, this could be nothing more than opportunistic and indiscriminate hoarding on Darboven's part, but the success of her work lies in the exactly filigreed minimum of sense that she laces—just barely present—through all the work's elements and traces from the past. Encountering *Cultural History 1880 - 1983*, you divine little pulses of patterns, hunches and forensic prompts that suggest (rather than prove) that there is some understanding close by, some understanding of the choppy, oceanic forces propelling twentieth-century Europe out of the nineteenth century and into the twenty-first.[4]

This word 'oceanic' helps us make some peace with a paradox that presently drives information cultures and their memory-systems. Applied to the study of archives, the 'oceanic' notion suggests the vastness, the dynamics and the intractability of all the data now proliferating in the self-recording world. Whereas archivists, librarians and indexers used to laud precision and comprehensiveness, it is a fact that the interpretable world presently evades all-encompassing lists and syntheses. Authoritative old forms such as the complete *catalogue raisonné* don't really catch and contain the sense of contemporary culture anymore; rather it is the log, that unending, polyglot report deriving from maritime culture that best connotes the seepage and uncontainability of data.

The cultural log is everywhere now, of course, in the millions of blogs blooming across the World Wide Web. One of the visionaries of archiving, Jay Leyda, brought the logging idea brilliantly into the humanities, in exuberant projects responding to the hoarded papers and effects of, firstly, Herman Melville and, later, Emily Dickinson. In his two-volume *Melville Log*, Leyda (who trained with Sergei Eisenstein) declares: 'I called what I was doing a Log of Melville's life, for my purpose was to record the essentials of that life's latitude and longitude, of its weather, course, whales captured or whales merely seen.'[5] Leyda looked for endless pulses and flows rather than for any locked mechanics of sure meaning: 'the relation between two documents, among a cluster of documents, tells us far more than we would ever have guessed by examining them singly. These invisible relationships speak not only of Melville but of the historical climate in which he worked and died'.[6] Leyda's method presaged Darboven's, particularly in the way they both seek to obliterate the didactic, hierarchical logic of the 'well-managed' collection, replacing this logic with a heuristic and associative impulse where every element is equally available to all others. Leyda's description of his Dickinson project (*The Years and Hours of Emily Dickinson*) could be Adler's account of Darboven's work: 'The reader should be prepared for the strangest possible variety of juxtaposed documents, transcribed and extracted from manuscripts and printed sources, ordered and dominated by a single chronology, and presented with a single aim: to get at the truth of Emily Dickinson.'[7] The more detail, the fuzzier the truth; but to discount the fuzziness would be to veer into fallacy.

In the same breath that I introduced the 'oceanic' idea earlier, I also mentioned the 'forensic' tendency. This drive to investigate and detect, to bring the secret or occult clue into the brighter light of the forum, is consonant with the urge to blog, to expose something obscure by bringing it to communal discourse.

The forensic impulse is everywhere in contemporary culture. The notion first chimed for me in the mid-1990s when I read Michael Joyce's cultural history of hypertext, *Of Two Minds*.[8] Early in the book, Joyce observes that hypertext is special because it is a means by which we can prioritise structural thought over serial thought. He explains how the linking, cross-referencing and branching allowed by hypertext have arisen to serve a readership that is really a forensic populace, a populace looking to take charge of their own conviction, looking to scheme, construct and test rather than to receive their worldview. This is a voluble, investigative audience that knows there are many variabilities and volatilities defining life now, so many that it is implausible to rely on the reception of one line of argument or explanation (which unfurls as serial thought), because the premises on which any one serial discourse is founded are always debatable and subject to rapid redundancy or mutation. By extension, the preference for structural and systematic thinking has emerged because of the old authorities broadcasting serial forms—be they newspapers, radio, television or parliamentary politics—that have repeatedly proven untrustworthy. Instead, many people now are always looking to assess a multi-dimensional array of propositions and repercussions associated with their every action in the world. No longer is the massed majority of people merely a conformity of 'consumers' who are ready to accept the singular delineation of effect-following-cause-following-effect-following-cause. Rather, an investigative audience wants to scan the field of lived and represented experience, triangulating the data, assaying the strengths, weaknesses, opportunities and threats prevailing in the dynamic complex of tendencies, mutations and options that constitute the life of today's somewhat free-willed but inextricably networked subjects.

This conundrum—the struggle for free will within a bureaucratic polis—is the theme of Sven Spieker's *The Big Archive: art from bureaucracy*. Spieker starts with the simple but resonant claim that the introduction of each new technology of communication has caused an emphatic shift in the culture of archiving. Compiling my own manifest as a way into Spieker's big idea, I can invite you to think of the arrival of pen-inscribed paper: to think of the telegraph, the typewriter, carbon paper, the telephone, the television, the tape recorder, the computer and online networks of interactive communication. It is an axiom in media studies that the moment after a new communications technology is invented someone asks 'How can this thing be used for sex?' Well, Spieker makes it clear that at the next heartbeat someone else is asking, 'And how can it be used for record-keeping?' (I am reminded here of Ann Laura Stoler's observation, acknowledging Max Weber, that the 'official secret' is the 'specific invention of bureaucracy'.[9])

Examining 'the way the bureaucratic archive shaped art practice in the twentieth century, from Dadaist montage to late-twentieth-century installation', Spieker shows how the animus in archive-culture is an unresolvable oscillation between chaos and classification, memory and speculation, trace and synthesis, metonym and metaphor.[10] All these tensions in bureaucratic governance have caused the twentieth century to fall under and then out of a spell entangling control and disintegration. This idea is borrowed from James Beniger, particularly from his contention that the Western world succumbed to a 'control revolution' during the period 1880–1930. 'Before this time,' Beniger contends, 'control of government and market had depended on personal relationships and face-to-face interactions' but the industrial revolution caused control to be 'reestablished by means of bureaucratic organization, [as well as by] the new infrastructures of transportation and telecommunications, and system-wide communication via the new mass media'.[11] Glossing Beniger, Spieker cuts to the chase that he needs for his tale:

> However, the technological means through which that control was established also carried with them an increased, yet largely unacknowledged, risk of an uncanny loss of control. The problem was that the office machines that came into widespread use between 1870 and 1920—from typewriters to card indexes—not only processed existing records at record speed, but also produced record amounts of new data.[12]

In sum, the control revolution was and is a continuing struggle for the massive manipulation of social memory—of the storage, retrieval and combinative activation of bits of old information. Which is why the archive books that I have cited here are also history books.

In addition to imagining erotic and bureaucratic uses for new communication technologies, early adopters tend to ask how the new gadgets can mess with time and with vernacular notions of past, present and immediate future. For example, think of how telegraph, CB radio, the VCR and YouTube all changed the way scheduling operated as soon as 'senders' and 'receivers' could use the new technologies to dispatch, store, search, replay and recombine packets of communication. Said most simply, with each of these new technologies people got *to wait* in new ways. Or, more precisely, many people figured out how to refuse the rhythms of waiting, withholding and doling out that are controlled by bureaucracies such as television stations or education systems.

Once the search-and-play function of an archiving system gets enhanced and democratised—especially through the use of computers—so that people can approach a critical mass of reposed material and expect to manipulate it with new and freshly powerful agency, then the control revolution takes a new turn. Localised and interpersonal transactions can then begin to reorganise labour and capital while industry and the state are forced to seek out new ways to constrain and channel the activities of the citizenry.

If you examine the ontology of such changefulness, you can see that all this happens around the segmenting, management and containment of time in relation to the recall of archived packets of information that govern peoples' contemplation and action. Next, if you append epistemology and politics to the ontology, familiarising yourself with the ability to timeshift and coupling this ability to powerful mechanisms for searching and pattern-recognition amidst accrued records (which are the *raison d'être* for computers), then the world really does lurch on to some new axes. On an interactive network, for example, you start to see rhythms of expectation, demand and action, pushing and pulling, spiralling, breaking and reforming through time, across space and across classes, work regimes and cultural activity. You might start to doubt positivist simplifications of evolutionary narratives in which the deficient past always gets outmoded by the efficient present; you might doubt broadcasts received; you might lose patience with hierarchies imposed and timetables arbitrarily delivered without widespread and continuous negotiation.

None of this necessarily means that some new social liberation is nigh. But old patterns of compliance do get shaken, at the very least. And the past and the present stutter across each other because everything stored is equally available for present-day consideration and for future recombination. The ancient past and the recent past lose their perspectival arraignment. Instead of lining up as an accession to contemporary command, all pasts *percolate through each other*, as the French mathematician and philosopher Michel Serres has said often in his career. Concomitantly, history loses its standard delineations of serial thought and takes new shapes, some of them dynamic, volumetric and curlicue, some of them viscous, some of them vaporous.

In such a swirling world, authority is not a given, not something simply thrust down upon the mess of raw data and disorganised citizenry. Rather, authority is just the contingency of influence and persuasive force shifting along a spectrum between language and military ordnance. In such a swirling world, authority is potentially everywhere, and it has to be proffered and found and constantly tested. And to the extent that it is operative anywhere, anytime, authority is always only momentarily affirmed by the people finding and negotiating all its componentry.

In the world of the dynamic and relational database, mastery over the three archival fundaments—content, indexing and synthesis—depends on the dexterity and reach of your searching. This is perhaps a fourth fundament—the search. Or, more exactly, it is a nimble and tireless ability to integrate the original three. The better your ability to search, the better your ability to speculate, test and understand by assembling past traces in any shifting moment. From memory comes proposition in the instant present, and from the next moment (the immediate future) come the testing and adjustment of that now-passing proposition.

In this flux there is new tumult for history makers. It is tumult brought by new matter, new mysteries, new forms of modelling the elements and valency of the past. It is clear now that this new history will no longer take predominantly a serial form. Outstripping Michael Joyce's vision, it will not even be structural. Rather, the new historiography will be dynamic and atmospheric, complex, on an edge of chaos, but tendency-governed and observable all the same. And it will accept that all past things are equally in contact, so long as you have the ability to store, index, search and synthesise with them.

In a recorded world built computationally upon relational archives, the new assumptions about history and memory (both psychological and social) are already lurking and looming. The big synthesising struggles rising out of such a world will be staged around the questions of who asserts ownership over the content-caches, questions about who orders and indexes the ways in to the content, and who has the best abilities for searching amidst the bolsters and barriers. If you have used Google today, you have already left some traces in the new histories and the new configurations of memory.

Notes
1 See N. Bourriaud, *Relational Aesthetics* Les presses du réel, Paris, 2002 (first published 1998); and N. Bourriaud, *Postproduction* Lukas & Sternberg, New York, 2002.
2 Quote from Emerson's classic essay 'Nominalist and Realist', cited in E. Cadava, *Emerson and the Climates of History*, Stanford University Press, Stanford, 1997, p. 60.
3 D. Adler, *Hanne Darboven: Cultural History 1880–1983*, Afterall Books,

London, n. d., received 2009, p. 2.
4   See Adler, pp. 2–5.
5   J. Leyda, *The Melville Log: a documentary life of Herman Melville 1819–1891*, Harcourt Brace and Company, New York, 1951, vol. 1, p. xii.
6   Leyda, *The Melville Log*, p. xii.
7   J. Leyda, *The Years and Hours of Emily Dickinson*, Archon Press, North Haven, CT, 1970 (first published 1960) p. xix.
8   See M. Joyce, *Of Two Minds: Hypertext Pedagogy and Poetics*, Ann Arbor: University of Michigan Press, Ann Arbor, 1995.
9   A. L. Stoler, *Along the Archival Grain: epistemic anxieties and colonial common sense*, Princeton University Press, Princeton, 2009, p. 26.
10 S. Spieker, *The Big Archive: art from bureaucracy*, The MIT Press, Cambridge, MA, 2008, p. 1.
11 J. R. Beniger, *The Control Revolution: technological and economic origins of the information society*, Harvard University Press, Cambridge, MA, 1986, p. 37.
12 Spieker, *The Big Archive*, p. 5.

5

EXTRACTIVE REALISM

Here is a fine haiku by the Japanese poet Seishi, a twentieth-century master:

> The signal pistol
> Echoes on the hard surface
> Of the swimming pool.[1]

And the tiny gem below is by the contemporary Australian writer Robert Gray, matching Seïshi for precision even though Gray's poem is fashioned from a larger and looser part of the world:

> Torpid farmland afternoons.
> A windmill stirs
> as a bubble breaks in buttermilk.[2]

Entire systems of reality are sketched quickly but exactly in these two quick utterances. Shifts of scale spring from quickly conjured settings. Sudden perspective-changes crack open the scenes. Conjunctions of heat and smell and sound all shuttle across your cognitive frame, putting you here and there in a flash, giving you sudden and intense access to extra realities within the settings that are being assayed. From the intimacy of your own witnessing body, you span out to encompass sharp details of large places—the hard acoustic slap in a swimming pool that is big enough for tournaments; the almost-imperceptible transpiration across flatland paddocks that need more water than raw nature supplies. And then in the next instant, as the meagre syllables slip along, memories pulse suddenly within you to bring you quickly back close to yourself (or to other selves within you) via past time. All this occurs in a rhythm that folds the larger world and you together. Appreciating Seishi's and Gray's crystalline miniatures, you know closeness as well as vastness in a retinue of glimmering instants. Emphasising definitive details of lived experience so exactly, both poems are realist.

Seishi once explained why utterances as tiny as these can be so thrilling, so revelatory. In an aside acknowledging his admiration of the French symbolist poets, he quoted Stéphane Mallarmé, asserting that '[because] objects are already in existence, it is not necessary to create them…all we have to do is grasp the relationships among them.'[3] This 'credo' from Mallarmé (which has become axiomatic for me and will turn up in later chapters of this book) chimes well with Thomas Hoover's previously cited account of what happens in a successful haiku: 'the mind is struck as with a hammer, bringing the senses up short and releasing a flood of associations.'[4] In the moment of intensified perception and interpretation that gets laid out across three concise lines, messy existence can be rendered as an essence so that the gist of an experience is offered as a refined set of organised elements and shaping influences that hold a larger world intensified on a page and poised to spring vast in your mind.

I remember being warned off traditional Japanese aesthetics in graduate school, when I was being trained to measure the political affordances in every cultural process and product. I recall being told that statements such as Hoover's and traditions such as Zen and the symbolist credos all peddled a belief in some illusory and immaterial essence that purports to float freely above the everyday struggles of citizens labouring in the messier world of material exigency. I remember being warned that aesthetes such as the old Zen masters and their modern apologists were just haughty Platonists wrapped up and suspended in false consciousness, uninterested in the material work that politics must bring to the real world, to the objective conflict zones of pragmatic action.

However, these condemnations missed the fact that immaterial *relationships* always insinuate the material componentry of the world; they missed that combinative influences are coursing constantly amidst all secular experience, and that such systems combine to cause reality. True, it is tempting to assert that some patrician or *ideal* state beyond politics has been extracted in these tiny poems, rarefied and diamantine as they appear. But it is misleading—perhaps it is fair to say it is *unreal*—to insist that these reduced impressions of habitable scenes are so refined as to be ineffable and depoliticised. When Thomas Hoover declared that a haiku can provide a quick metaphysical jolt that helps a reader discern some connective valence in the everyday world, he was not arguing for aesthetical transcendence beyond political affairs. Rather he was describing how the reader can be brought dramatically close into the often covert connectivity that subtends and really arranges the world.

Granted, I have spent these opening paragraphs chasing some esoteric concerns, but by clarifying this notion of *the extract* I have found a useful way to start thinking about 'the art of the real', particularly as it can be practised in my own society.

Australia—my own society—is a nation where much has depended on concealment: think of the land-grabbing, think of the withholding of payments and wages to Indigenous workers, think of the reluctance to acknowledge the damage that has been caused by water wastage, carbon emissions and by imported systems of land use. In such a society it is profitable to deploy the trope of *the extract* provocatively, because a well-chosen detail can act as the startling trigger that releases the flood of associations for anyone who has been primed to perceive what lies beneath the surface of ordinary experience. An extracted detail might grant a focused observer access to the systematic understanding of a larger reality.

Next question: how to perfect the extractive method and thereby turn oneself and one's readers into focused observers? First answer: I can begin to exemplify the method with brief reference to three projects from my own research.

Example 1: For many years I have been ruminating on the enigmatic notebooks of marine lieutenant William Dawes, who recorded weather conditions and astronomical patterns as well as a small but hugely significant fraction of Indigenous vocabulary and grammar in the Sydney Cove district during his tour of duty in the military takeover of the country between 1788 and 1791.[5] The evidence in the taciturn notebooks is truncated because Dawes was sent home to England just as he was beginning to grasp and extract the nameable components (vocabulary) and the essential organising principles (grammar) of the local language. What we have to work with, therefore, is a partial set of intensely significant clues and *a world of absences* across which we must speculate imaginatively yet rigorously. In Dawes' notebooks, a flood of associations can flow, but the reader needs to learn how to strike hammers on the limited set of keys that have survived the past via the lieutenant's meagre transcriptions. In doing so, the reader is trained to sense the relationships that held the world together even as it was beginning to fall apart. The reader is trained to understand the world of Sydney Cove *relationally* and always *provisionally*, with a postulative understanding that is constantly in process.

Example 2: Late last century I wrote *Seven Versions of an Australian Badland*. It examines a landscape where colonial land-grabbing and monocultural farming have plundered the environment until the place now appears like a defiled and exhausted thing. Over the past five decades I have crossed this broken country many times, with a growing conviction that it is a scree of evidence bearing witness to the unruly historical forces that have shaped it. In such landscapes—and they are everywhere in Australia—we have to ask, what can be made of this scene now? Attending to relationships amongst a constrained array of details that were highlighted through the selective and combinative procedure of my writing in *Seven Versions*, I nudged the reader into asking questions. For example, what can we know about the ecologies that have gone feral in Central Queensland? What of the wrenched geomorphics, the weed-infested gullies and floodplains, the roofless towns with a dozen residents still hanging about? How can we overhear the pertinent gossip, the attempts at truth, the self-serving lies? What of the journey-patterns, the trekking rhythms cross-hatching the country together with time, now meshed in the past? What can we make of the documents that have been generated in response to this country? And what of the absences blotting the retrieved documentary evidence: when are they significant, when are they negligible? In *Seven Versions* I tried to use all the scrappy details to help people think about the absences and silences that stretch between all the pinpointed examples that made up the scenarios that I presented in prose that was deigned to spur rigorous speculation rather than to lock down singular conclusions.

Example 3: In this example, a series of computer-activated works of audio-visual art known collectively as *Life After Wartime*—viewers are given textual and musical prompts encouraging them to account for a salvaged batch of crime-scene photographs that no longer have any conclusive documents attached.[6] As *Life After Wartime* has grown, project by project, a cluster of imaginative and analytical responses to the photographs have aggregated into a database that works as a kind of story-engine proffering an infinite set of plausible but inherently contentious and restless speculations concerning the enigmatic scenes in the archive. Here is one little sample from the *Life After Wartime* suite, an excerpt from a long online picture-poem called *Accident Music*:

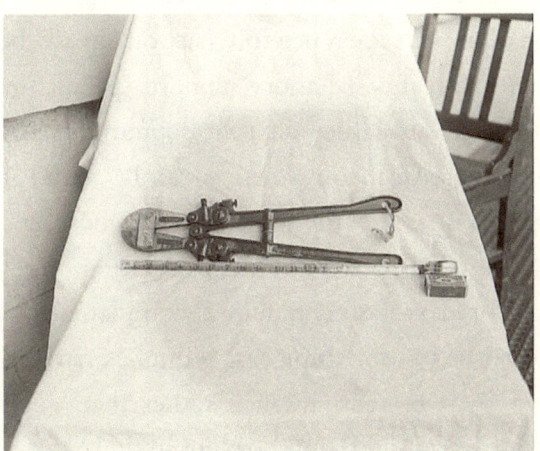

*Everything is worth something — Make rust with blood —
A fact, blunt and material — Fluid on a breadboard & a smear on the doorstep —
You might wash your hands all morning, but they'll never be clean again.*

In each of these three examples selected from my research portfolio, I try to draw some relational understanding out across a sparse array of vestigial evidence. I try to show how worlds that are usually riddled with concealment and absence can be provisionally and provocatively highlighted and integrated so that, in a flash of connective apprehension, people engaging with the work might know more fully the forces and flows that truly prevail in whatever reality the extracts come from. The details of the extracts carry some impress of their originating reality; and for all their aspiration to fictional 'panache', the artworks that get brewed from the details still display a staunch allegiance to something real. They are less fictional than they are realistically obliged.

There is a quality of *restlessness* crucial to these artistic investigations. By restlessness, I mean the way an artwork—be it a book, a database, a building, a garden—can activate your imagination by offering to your mind a system of artful imbalances and implied possibilities that are available for patterned completion inside your own imagination with reference to what you already believe to be tested and true in reality. Memory supports speculation.

As I noted in an earlier chapter, supreme examples of this aesthetic of generative incompleteness can be found in Zen temples and gardens, where the visitor experiences environments that seem 'charged' with a powerful integrating 'urge', a flowing potentiality for as-yet-unconcluded completeness. The urge presses in response to something that is implied rather than shown, absent rather than present, implicit rather than explicit. To be precise, the urge arises in the visitor; not in the environment. The visitor often feels compelled to imagine a pattern cohering across and around the essential elements and the artful absences that have been offered or extracted for appreciation. Even though the larger pattern is not patently present in the deliberately 'unresolved' space (or time, if the artwork is a piece of music or designed sound), it is available to the imagination because the abstemious offering of extracts prompts in the viewer an aesthetic yearning to complete the inherent pattern. This yearning often helps the viewer feel inseparable from the environment, to feel responsible for and attuned to some flowing integrity in the domain under consideration.[7]

In Zen treatises this connective drive is often called *ma*, the word given to the fuzzy sense of potentiality that lurks and is ready to be made manifest, under the right conditions, in all spaces through time.[8] Applied to contemporary Western experience, it might be dubbed *the forensic impulse*. This compulsion to bring latent factors into the public view of the *forum* (hence the adjective *forensic*) seems to be ubiquitous now in popular culture. Much verbiage could be spent arguing how distrust of the illusory surfaces skinning contemporary political and commercial confabulations has recently strengthened a vernacular desire to see behind the scenes and to draw covert processes out from concealment. Clearly this crisis in governmentality coincides with the emergence of online and interactive communication networks which allow citizens to seek out and 'triangulate' their knowledge and to coordinate their agit-prop campaigns (think of getup.org.au; think of reddit.com) instead of passively receiving information in one uninterrupted flow of edited and self-interested opinion.

In such a restless world, never-ending scepticism gets aligned to continuous, rigorous postulation. It is a creative rather than a cynical impulse. Moreover, in schools and universities there is a shift away from the expectation that citizens are merely receptive. And the sceptical attitude coincides with a general abandonment of didactic modes of teaching, to be replaced by the heuristic or discovery-based mode that encourages students into guided learning that is stimulated by intrigue and by the careful priming of essential clues prompting students into further inquiry. (In PowerPoint shorthand, this shift is usually glossed as 'The Sage on the Stage gives way to The Guide Alongside'.) Scholars and citizens are encouraged to become detectives seeking out an ever-broadening array of hammers for their minds. Attuned to this heuristic mentality, many *artists* are drawn similarly to resonant details, to essences and extracts that are designed to enhance active speculation about the ever-emerging world that is available for intervention.

Having pondered and practised this 'aesthetic of the detail' for a couple of decades now, I've begun to understand how to weld some of my late-acquired insights about the haiku onto yet another strand of criticism that I encountered at graduate school, namely the realist analyses of the great Hungarian critic Georg Lukács. Whereas I once would have expected the two approaches to cancel each other out, I can appreciate the poetry in Lukács' Marxism more readily now, just as I can see the sly politics in the Japanese aesthetics.

In Lukács' bravura essay 'Narrate or Describe', he sets out a distinction between realism (which he admires and endorses because of its active and revelatory narrative qualities) and naturalism (which he finds alluring but diverting and suspect in its descriptive enthralment). Lukács conscripts the work of Emile Zola and Leo Tolstoy to illustrate his polemic. Zola exemplifies an alienating style of naturalism because the novelist is too adroit at petit-pointing details in a compositional process whereby intricate scenes get '*described* from the standpoint of an observer'. By contrast, Tolstoy purveys a vital and stimulating realism because he always hacks out definitive aspects and grabs the key vectors inside dynamically evolving scenes that are '*narrated* from the standpoint of a participant'.[9] This selective and active realism causes a kind of Zen *satori,* an awakening blow to the mind of the reader who tags alongside the narrator and gets inside the generative core of the scenes. I like to think of it this way:

naturalism is *additive* and it diffuses focus as more and more details are supplied; which means that realism, by contrast, is bolder and more useful than naturalism because realism is *extractive* in the way it draws out and exposes the definitive, structuring elements of a scene. Whereas naturalist art casts an appreciative light on surfaces concealing a deeper reality, realist art helps us to probe into the reasons and to feel the shaping forces subtending reality.

Here is the connection back to the haiku and to the examples from my own research, which were cited earlier in this chapter. In the Lukácsian mode of realism, because it is extractive, artists are determined to shuck away extraneous detail so they can learn how the *relationships between essential elements* all cohere contingently to make the overall, dynamic experience that is everyday existence. With realist works, the artist and the audience engage in a forensic process, seeking out and extracting the key, formative elements or clues that will lead to fuller, more causal understanding of the scenes being represented.

Now rather than risking too much subjectivity by propounding more examples from my own portfolio, let's exemplify this practice of extractive realism more exactly by examining an artform that might at first seem misplaced here: Jamaican dub music. For me, alongside the centuries-old tradition of the haiku, dub is the other great example of essence-aesthetics, even though the art form is barely four decades old. One of the finest practitioners was Osbourne Ruddock, a.k.a. King Tubby (1941–89). Tubby produced thousands of remarkable tracks. A brief soundscape by him, called *Version Dub*, is one masterpiece among many. It is worth describing and analysing closely, to show how Lukács' literary insights might be ported over to help with realist appreciations of other media.

In less than three minutes, *Version Dub* builds a world, sets a stage, and on that stage Tubby arrays a set of powerful feelings and conducts a subtle argument about history, art and the place of subjects (be they vociferous, be they voiceless) within the legacy of colonialism and slavery. The tune commences with a quiet cymbal stutter that sounds like wind agitating seedy gourds hanging off jungle vines. This dry rattle lasts exactly one second before it gets settled by electric guitar that is highly reverberant almost pedal steel, but more peppy with jazz tonics that stretch singing over a sonic bed of crackly distortion pushing up through the top registers. This crackle is no accident or problem in the mix. It is meant to be there. It might be the inserted sound of a stylus grooving on degraded vinyl or it might be grain in the ferrous oxide of magnetic tape that has been deliberately dubbed and over-dubbed and amplified a dozen times or more until the producer has heard and logged the 'trouble' he has in mind. There is wow and flutter in there too, purposefully included. As soon as we have understood all this, we get a few beats more of the grit, and then we hear some drawly, massed brass instruments blowing underneath the guitar, pushing between the plucked strings and the crackle. And now a bassline settles in—solid, dry, with no reverb in this last burr of the sound.

Thus with the tune only twenty seconds old, Tubby has already sketched out a space for us: the reverb accords dimensions to a sonic world that has audible boundaries, the crackle puts a dirty ground under us, the bass gives a dependable schedule and encourages trust that this ground will hold while, now and then, the cymbals will agitate and the horns will blow a flitting breeze that measures the atmospheric pressure. This world is an aural island of some kind, with edges, resonance, humidity and a localised sense of time and tone.

But is the island populated? Yes! There it is at the 30-second mark: a falsetto vocal gulp. An emotional utterance rather than a semantic statement, this gulp anticipates Michael Jackson's yelps in *Billie Jean* but it also harks way back to African singing techniques as well as Carribean church music and early American R&B crooners like Sonny Til from the Orioles.[10] Clearly, the human voice has a place in Tubby's world. Into his ever thickening soundscape, he has dropped this startling ululation by Yabby You, a vocalist renowned for silky melodies that smuggle politically and spiritually 'conscious' messages across to the local 'sufferahs'. Constrained and intensified, the sound might be anguish or it might be rapture. Of course, in Tubby's world it is both: the two connotations are complementary as well as contradictory.

Then, as if in response to Yabby's call, we get a barely audible and deliberately thin and degraded skerrick of choral singing—perhaps it is an ensemble of singers, or perhaps it is one voice re-copied several times upon itself to form a slightly out-phased harmonic. This sound is not words you can decipher; rather it is a vocalised, aestheticised echo that has been conjured and shaped in response to the first voice. These 'answering' voices are a long way back in the mix, as if coming from across a river, off in a yonder valley, or drifting over the sea from out past the horizon. The distant call wafts a couple more times and then Tubby pulls all the environing sound down almost to zero for a moment so that in this lull he lets the faraway voices register unchallenged, as if they are carried on a pushing breeze or in a momentary wave of liberated radio transmission.

Only fifty seconds into the song now, we have an aesthetic model of Jamaica—not just the geography, ecology and atmosphere of the island but also its history and ideology. Hearing the sound from the inside, from the standpoint of a participant and an inhabitant, we experience an extracted model of this place where absence is a defining feature, where influences drift in partially and perennially over the horizon, where radio programs come and go from Florida, Cuba and the coast of Texas. We can sense how, in this place of traces, the ancient indigenes have long been obliterated and the contemporary inhabitants are migrants always searching for orientation, always harking back in memory to some elsewhere in their heads and hearts, even as they know that *this place here* is their lot now, that they have no other home to make but here. With the aesthetics of seepage and submergence, with the entangled mnemonics and amnesia that define dub music, we hear and feel the silence, exile and cunning that often define a migrant's life.

One and a half minutes into the song, the 'sound weather' that Tubby has been concocting finds its full, stealthy shape. And straight away the song begins to form its finish. The distant voices are quickly engulfed again by the drums and horns, louder than ever, making a swell of larger elements momentarily washing over the human presence in this world of restless sound. Bringing the tune home now, Tubby waits for the symphonics to lull once more, wavelike, before cuing the humanity one last time. The voice resurfaces nearby and the guitar, horns and drums slowly ebb with the diminishing vocals till the entire composition goes down to a kind of sun-setting silence thickening all around the listener.

What strengthens, as the song wanes, is the notion that *Version Dub* is a sonic island, closely and sensually modeled on an actual island. The tune is realist, therefore. From the reverb we can estimate the scope of the world. From the crackle we get a haptic sense of how that world might grip. From the emerging and submerging insinuations of the different melodies, we sense the dynamics flushing through this domain made of sound. It is as if we are left hearing, as inhabitants and participants from the inside, an exquisite abstraction of the geography and fecundity of Tubby's kingdom. Which is both a fantastic and a real place.

To the extent that the song refers to the drift and decay of radio transmissions emanating from Florida and Cuba, it is a quick lesson in international relations. There's that word again: relations. It links us back to the haikus with which we commenced this chapter. And it helps us bring the argument to a close. The poetry of Seishi and Gray and the music of Tubby all extract intensified reality through the same process: instantaneous, immersed perception is interwoven with volatile, voluptuous remembrance, altogether releasing that now-familiar flood of associations. Like a condensed guide to a globalising existence, Tubby's tune offers a sensory commentary on the memory-waste, the associative rumination and the institutional thought-policing that abrade any migrant's attempt to find a home or a voice in any place, new or old, where one might need to establish an identity founded not on righteous origins but on ingenuity and persistence. Displacement, persistence, ingenuity, changefulness, remembrance; these real elements have been rendered into art that can orient you.

Version Dub is a plangent thesis explaining how the modern consciousness is inevitably a variable work in progress, something that has to be asserted and endlessly earned and performed moment by moment in negotiation with prevailing conditions. Not 'grounded' in a homeland—the modern consciousness cannot rely on myths that celebrate how people can *arise* from their original, hosting soil; instead the modern citizen tends to *arrive* and *survive* in a place where no birthright is readymade. Hence the defining and completely pertinent sense of erasure and incompletion in dub, the sense of a musical form in which utterance competes with voicelessness, where agency contends with anonymity. And hence the 'X-ray' quality of this music, the way it is built from extracts and underlying hints that grant the listener a clearer apprehension of the formative elements or structuring skeleton within the tangled contemporary world.[11]

Tubby's compositions are forensic and Lukácsian therefore, in the way they extract and emphasise the previously covert principles that organise the real place that he represents. Having made this link with Lukácsian realism, we can bring the chapter full-circle to its close now by noting how Tubby's music is useful and inspiring in a way that matches Seishi's and Gray's poems: all these artworks are poetically forensic and extractively realist; they inkle out the resonant details and the immaterial relations that really matter, that galvanise a scene and keep the artist and the audience allied to reality. In this tense but thrilling interplay between the urge to select and the urge to combine, the artist can make sure that a provocative, contentious, continuous and pinpoint-efficient realism is always playing out extractively.

In a globalised, saturated world of networked glut, realism like this can be a beacon. In its brevity and speculative association, this extractive but active realism helps us find some way to maintain our allegiance to the world of everyday experience. As another of Gray's miniature poems says:

> The world, it seems, is the maximum
> Number of things, or of forces,
> That can exist together.[12]

To know this world properly we need art that lets us comprehend just the right amount of extracted things and forces that can relate well together. Realistically, we need to be in the midst of only what is essential. No more details than that.

Notes

1. R. H. Blyth, *A History of Haiku*, vol. II, Hokuseido Press, Tokyo, 1964, p. 346.
2. R. Gray, 'Twenty Poems', in *Selected Poems 1963–1983*, Angus & Robertson, Sydney, 1985, p. 91.
3. Y. Seishi, *The Essence of Modern Haiku*, Mangajin, Atlanta, 1993 p. xix.
4. T. Hoover, *Zen Culture*, Routledge & Kegan Paul, London, 1978 p. 205.
5. See R. Gibson, *26 Views of the Starburst World: William Dawes at Sydney Cove 1788–91*, UWAP, Perth, 2012.
6. This is a long-running collaborative project with Kate Richards. See www.lifeafterwartime.com.
7. See, for example, N. Carver, *Form and Space of Japanese Architecture*, Shokokusha, Tokyo, 1955, p. 156. Carver explains that in Zen architecture, 'all relationships are abbreviated and subtle, encouraging the exercise of the imagination in grasping the whole'.
8. See G. Nitschke, '"MA": the Japanese sense of "place" in old and new architecture and planning', in *Architectural Design*, March 1966, p. 117.
9. G. Lukács, A. Kahn (trans. and ed.), *Writer and Critic and other Essays*, Merlin Press, London, p. 111.
10. Listen especially to Sonny Til's keening in 'It's Too Soon to Know' (1948) on the audio CD *Sonny Til and the Orioles, Greatest Hits*, the Collectables Label, 1991.
11. M. E. Veal, *Dub: soundscapes and shattered songs in Jamaican Reggae*, Wesleyan University Press, Middletown, CT, 2007, p. 196. Veal acknowledges Luke Erlich and Lee Perry as the sources of the 'X-ray' description.
12. R. Gray, 'Epigrams' in *New Selected Poems*, 2nd edition, Duffy & Snellgrove, Sydney, 1998, p. 296.

6

SPIRIT HOUSE

Wonder

This essay ponders the wonder-full sense of remembrance you sometimes feel when visiting a museum. Do you know this sensation? Partly, it is a feeling of care for the artefacts on display. More precisely, it is a *structure of feeling*, a carefully composed configuration of intrigues and affirmations moving you and moving through you when you contemplate the system of objects and propositions laid out in the galleries.[1] More than just the apprehension of meanings in the displays, it is a feeling of *involvement* with all the emotive forces generated in you by the entire array of the exhibits. It is a palpable sense of being absorbed and altered by everything on offer when you are engaged as much by the textures, heft and scale of the materials as by their curatorially determined significance. And because you feel the museum getting into you somehow, you sense a burgeoning responsibility for the material on display. You care for the exhibits as you would for yourself and you want to comprehend how the museum is defining and expanding your sense of self, how you're getting this sensation of a real, historical continuum folding into yourself, past into present, through these artefacts.

An example: I always get this curious urge when I visit the Pitt Rivers Museum in Oxford. A wonderstruck knot of emotions and hunches cinches inside me as I feel the acquisitive lust, the surreal ravaging of meaningful categories, and the catastrophic displacements and realignments that were enacted by colonialism across the globe. Moving amidst the massed displays, I get some sense too of the vivacious originating cultures that produced the singular marvels that are recontextualised so astonishingly in the museum's great glass-roofed chamber. By adhering to the typological 'logic' of General Pitt Rivers' taxonomic principles, the museum's curators make sure that several sense-making systems from Europe, Africa, Asia, Oceania and beyond are all put in contention and made just a little more palpable because of how startling most of the conjunctions feel. Without fail, I always get shocked *bodily* by the tangles of shape, size, colour and provenance that are so provocatively assembled all around me in the Pitt Rivers Museum, as thousands of musical instruments, for example, press against the innumerable weapons, cooking utensils, love charms and 'fetishes'.

Memory-places like the Pitt Rivers are made vivacious by the organising force of their combined somatic and semantic systems. So disturbing, so stimulating, such places are *inspired*, which is to say they are suffused with an activating and integrating spirit the same way a living body must have breath in it: the way anything vital is always inspiring, expiring, respiring.

After all, 'spirit' and 'breath' are words for each other. It is in this context that a successful museum can be regarded as a 'spirit house', a place made lively by a flowing, connective, integrative force that can be felt by a visitor encountering the somatic and semantic configurations arrayed in it.

Thus museums can be more than just representative models of the world, more than just secondary commentaries on primary experience. Rather, because of the way their artists and curators can select and conjoin particular aspects and artefacts from lived experience, the social and sensory constructs called museums can offer *intensifications* of the world's vitality. A museum can give you the chance to discern vivacious aspects of experience that are usually too obscure or attenuated to be well apprehended in the 'outside world'. A single exhibit can be a kind of 'pressure-chamber' or 'force field'. And the overall system of exhibits can channel some of these pressurised or focused forces so that we can discern how something vital and persistent can move through our shared world of space, matter, labour, passion and time.

The sensory power of exhibits is crucial to museology. Granted, the structured *feelings* that a museum can give you are not necessarily more important than the *information* that you might garner. But if the feelings are missing, if there is no sensory, breath-changing involvement, then people are not roused to care about the exhibits, and the museum won't have fully succeeded, for the visitors will not have undergone any transformative relationship to the world that has been intensified by the system of artefacts. This transformation is a palpable, somatic response that cannot be readily decoded like a message or a batch of data. Not entirely reasonable, this transformative urge is a *passion*: an event that *passes* through the visitor's sensibilities while artefacts and people and timescales fold into one another and alter one another within the overall patterning of the museum.

How might one become more adept at installing and 'channeling' this transformative feeling? How might we harness it for the purposes of more affecting and effective museological display? This feeling, which I have described as 'somatic' a couple of times already, is precisely an *aesthetic* concern rather than a semantic one.

Aesthetics is literally a field of study concerned with whatever is 'perceptible by the senses'.[2] When studying museum aesthetics, you try to comprehend how the senses can be engaged and enriched in a curated display that causes an organised urge to move through the perceiver.

Pondering all this, I have learned that some overlooked aspects of film theory are useful. Also snippets of unorthodox architectural theory make some sense, along with portions of Indigenous Australian philosophy. I have a hunch that it is feasible to combine all these in an attempt to understand the experience of wonder in museums, to see what this trans-disciplinary melding might yield.

We can start with the film theory.

Sunspots

In 1960 the French journal *Cahiers du cinema* published a brilliant essay called 'Sunspots', by a young Iranian scholar named Fereydoun Hoveyda.[3] (We will return to 'Sunspots' in greater detail in a later chapter of this book.) Hoveyda explains that cinema works best when it captures and channels an ever-unfolding force that runs through the spaces, objects and temporal rhythms of a film and also through the audience in the dark room. When a film really works, he explains, some kind of energy pulses coherently in space, in time and in people so that the organising energy of the scene flares through all the components of an individual shot and then arcs like electricity from shot to shot, from moment to moment, from screen to audience and back again. This is the 'mise en scène' of the film, the manner in which space and time are manipulated to make a special place for the viewer. The way mise en scène works is that a charge is generated that carries, excites and transforms every portion of the filmic experience. Characters, objects, spaces, luminance, time patterns and viewers all get altered as the aesthetics and semantics play out during a cinematic session. The film can thus be seen and *felt* to be an animated system where all things can be shown to have vitality in them and must therefore be considered part of each other somehow.

These notions are similar to the theories of 'suture' and 'enmeshment' that arose in film theory during the 1970s, for example in the writings of Jean-Pierre Oudart, Daniel Dayan and Stephen Heath.[4] Analysing how editing works in character-based narrative cinema, 'suture theory' describes how the viewer is purposefully shifted through several points of view and alignments of identification. As these different vantages on the represented world line up, the viewer's subjectivity is repeatedly cut and re-stitched, causing in the viewer a sensation of being commingled with the many characters, objects and spaces that have been presented through the unspooling sequence of the film. Viewers feel the film's systematic, organising force moving through them, stitching them into the larger body of the film's dynamic universe. Understand a film to be the compendium of all its characters, settings, moods and sounds. Consider the viewer and the film coming together and binding to each other in the theatre: each moves through the other, each gets into the other. A holistic sensation develops as one views the films, conjoining yourself with the characters, props, lighting patterns, sonic designs, movement surges and so on. No one element in the film, yourself included, can be construed as separate from or superior to the others. Each needs the other because every element in the experience is energising all the other elements.

Synthesis

In recent times, the practice of ecology has helped us understand how an interconnecting energy might weave through space and time so that the definitions of what is inert and what is alive must undergo extensive redefinition. Many cultures give spirit names to an animating force that binds places, things and rhythms into the lively world. Now, I am not so pantheist as to insist that there is a quantifiable life force in all the objects that comprise the world. There may be, but it is not crucial to the museological argument that I am developing here. The key point is that in an aesthetically designed environment an urge seems to flow through and from each object because of an energy generated within the senses of the people encountering the objects. It is a *psychic* energy that can become a *social* energy. Attending a film, for example, the viewer's communal affections are intensified firstly by the ritual of gathering in the auditorium and then by the crowd's collective attention, after undergoing the dimming down of the houselights, to the shuttling interweave of rhythm, luminance, scale, sound and language all passing through yourself and through your benighted fellows in the irradiated theatre.

Determined to be thoroughly secular about Hoveyda's fabled energy, I keep coming back to the 'Sunspots' essay because it helps me understand not only cinema but also installation art and museum exhibition. Moreover, Hoveyda's ideas about integrative energy and spectatorship link with some notions in Indigenous Australian philosophy and metaphysics. From recent times, one of the most inventive examples of adaptive Indigenous thinking comes from the late David Mowaljarlai, who spent the final twenty years of his life creating a spiritual system—pragmatic, ethical, ecological—that he was determined to communicate to non-Indigenous Australians.[5] (Note how Mowaljarlai keeps turning up as guide in these chapters. His work is proving evermore important as the decades roll by.) This system was based on ritual knowledge stored in his country in northwestern Australia. Mowaljarlai asserted that the country has psychic, social, geological and botanical life all synthesised into a vitality that guides a person to sensible actions. Literally sensible. Literally activated in the senses. Mowaljarlai described how he could feel the presence (or not), the valence (or not), the direction (or dissipation) of this country-vitality and he described how he could act in communion with this vitality. He could find spots in space and moments in time where the urgency in country is intensified, where this force signals most emphatically. He could sense the land's animus 'swinging' around him. This was no mystical ability. He could attune to this animus because of all the cultural work he had already performed, all the ritual tale-telling and remembering, all ceremonies that he enacted to frame and intensify the force in the country. This attunement was the result of relentless cultural labour—marking the ground, lodging painted figures in caves, determining sightlines to other sacred zones, bouncing songs off cliff faces. In other words, he was constantly arranging a mise en scène of country and from that mise en scène he was getting his cues for action, taking direction from the scene, flowing with the swinging energies of the scene because countless ancestors have already fashioned the country into a kind of sense-generator that he could cleave to.[6]

Forcefields

One would expect Mowaljarlai and Hoveyda to understand good portions of each other's beliefs. And one would expect them to respond well to the ideas of French architect and philosopher Bernard Cache, as expressed in his startling book *Earth Moves*. Cache declares that architecture is best understood as 'a cinema of things'.[7] Interlocking a set of directive frames, Cache explains, an architect works more with dynamics than with status, more like a film director than a builder. An architect channels the continuous flow of light and sound in consort with the trajectories of objects and people all moving in time and space so that every component of the built environment becomes implied and available to all the others. Every object, surface, sheet of light, potential trajectory, vault of air and volume of sound gets integrated in an aesthetically complete environment which is felt as a dynamic, flowing experience in the sensorium of everyone inhabiting and appreciating that environment.

Amplifying Cache's provocations, Elizabeth Grosz has suggested that architecture can be regarded as the primary art, because its frames are applied to preternatural forces.[8] The act of constructing a wall forms a floor, thus transforming raw ground into something domestic, making cultural order from the given, Adamite chaos. A soffit emphasises the built shelter of a roof combining with a wall to parry the attack of the prevailing elements streaming down from the cosmos. Think of the frame around a window as a focusing device that directs the trajectories not only of light and wind but also of eyesight. A directional cairn of stones might show travellers how to bring a sense of optimism as well as a river toward them while making tracks through a savannah. Grosz describes architecture as a process whereby space gets rendered lively so long as the architect harnesses and organises the tendencies both within the citizens and within the territory that is being constructed for them. One can extrapolate that architecture can do for space what social history and personal memory do for time – providing momentum, preserving, framing and shaping unstable experience, exposing and harnessing the world's tendencies and dynamic potentialities.

Seen like this, Cache's conception of a world made by architecture is close to Hoveyda's vision of cinema's integrated and irradiated universe. Which is close also to what museum exhibits can do for artefacts and interpretations. In a museum exhibit, the material world can be arrayed and interpreted so that an organised, aesthetic spirit connects and excites people in relation to places, timescales and objects.

Dylan Thomas once wrote of 'the force that through the green fuse drives the flower'.[9] This force is like the energy detected by Hoveyda, Mowaljarlai, Cache and Grosz, and it is comparable, I think, to the stimulation that one can feel in 'spirited' museum exhibits. Or as Nicolas Bourriaud's influential book *Relational Aesthetics* has proposed, contemporary museums are most relevant to everyday life when they help visitors grasp not the essential material qualities of the displays but the full potential of relations amongst people and artefacts. In the arrangement of these relations one sets right conditions for generating propositions and feelings.[10] As Bourriaud argues, museums can set up scenes where negotiations can occur, where people can feel secure enough to speculate about the associations and the affections required to make sense in a world where all the constituent parts exist in a constantly altering forcefield of power and possibility, a world shivered by globalisation, ecological change and accelerating accretions of recursive information gyrating in electronic communication networks.

So to bring the inquest of this chapter to summation, I would like to make an exhibit here on the page, an exhibit of the visions that we have generated in this essay. It is a way of relating the various theories of Mowaljarlai, Cache *et al.* Each brief definition is a separate but related vision of a vivacious museum. We can arrange them as an ensemble, as if in a showcase, to see whether they make sense for us; to see if they correlate to give us a cogent feeling about what a museum can be.

Here then, to finish the chapter, is my little exhibit of definitions all flowing in and out of each other. Might they conjure ideas and feelings of a museum worth visiting?

Museum: a place where we can assay the moving forces organising the world of matter, power, remembrance and feeling.

> **Museum:** a place secure enough, imaginative enough to help us trace lines connecting the existing and the potential relations amongst all aspects of our shared experiences of space and time, past and present.

Museum: a place where the vivacity in our built cultures can be shown to be collaborating with all our given natures.

> **Museum:** a place where the breath of the world can be intensified so that it can be discerned and transferred to all others interested.

Museum: a spirit house.

Notes
1 R. Williams, *Marxism and Literature*, Oxford University Press, Oxford, 1977, pp. 128–35.
2 G. A. Wilkes and W. A. Krebs (eds), *Collins English Dictionary*, 3rd edition, Harper Collins, Sydney, 1991, p. 24.

3   See J. Hillier (ed.), *Cahiers du cinéma, 1960–1968: New Wave, New Cinema, Re-evaluating Hollywood*, Harvard University Press, Cambridge, MA, 1986, pp. 135–45.
4   See J. Oudart, 'Cinema and Suture', *Screen* vol. 18 no 4, winter 1977/8, pp. 35–47; D. Dayan, 'The Tutor-Code of Classical Cinema', *Film Quarterly*, fall 1974, pp. 22–31; and S. Heath, 'On Suture' in his *Questions of Cinema*, Indiana University Press, Bloomington, 1981, pp. 76–112.
5   See D. Mowaljarlai and J. Malnic, *Yorro Yorro: everything standing up alive*, Magabala Books, Broome, 1993.
6   D. Mowaljarlai, ABC Radio Feature, 'The Law Report', Tuesday 31 October, 1995 http://www.abc.net.au/rn.
7   B. Cache, *Earth Moves: the furnishing of territories*, MIT Press, Boston, MA, 1995, p. 29.
8   E. Grosz, 'Chaos, Territory, Art, Deleuze and the Framing of the Earth', in *IDEA Journal 2005*, edited by S. Attiwill and G. Lee, Brisbane, 2005, pp. 15–25.
9   D. Thomas, 'The Force that through the Green Fuse Drives the Flower', in D. Jones (ed.), *Dylan Thomas: the poems*, J.M. Dent, London, 1974, p. 77.
10 N. Bourriaud, *Relational Aesthetics,* Les Presses du reel, Paris, 2002.

7

THE PULSE IN THE PAST

The human mind...operates by association. With one item in its grasp, it snaps instantly to the next that is suggested by the association of thoughts, in accordance with some intricate web of trails carried by the cells of the brain. It has other characteristics, of course; trails that are not frequently followed are prone to fade, items are not fully permanent, memory is transitory.

Vannevar Bush, 'As We May Think',
first published in *The Atlantic Monthly*, July 1945

Preamble

Memories emerge and submerge in the restive flux of consciousness. They are basic to personality, to history and therefore to culture. In the service of civic consciousness, archives hold prompts for memories. But artefacts in archives have rarely moved, converged, submerged and re-emerged as memories do. At least not until recently. But now digital and networked systems have begun to allow the stored parts of archives to associate and amalgamate via activeness and rhythms that not only mimic but also prompt the associative alchemy of historically informed understanding. As a cultural form and a psychological stimulant, the archive has been roused by digital systems.

Which brings us to the questions that guide this chapter. In mobilising archival material within digital systems, how can we access and appreciate the stored records in ways that activate our remembering consciousness not only with the poised consideration of intellect but also with the urgency of emotion? How can archives be truly moving? How can they be used not as repositories but as stimulant events? And how might archives exercise the motile, relational systems of memory, instead of just freezing and storing its miscellaneous componentry?

Whodunits

In his classic ethnography *Detective Work: a study of criminal investigations*, William Sanders notices that police tend to assume there are only two kinds of crimes: walkthroughs and whodunits. With walkthroughs, the perpetrator (who is usually a romantic associate if not a relative, workmate or neighbour of the victim) is deemed obvious, and the conviction is quick and simple. Most investigators start every case by looking for the walkthrough.[1] Indeed, almost every cop insists on it. Life gets challenging and exhausting when a walkthrough slides over, usually after three or four fruitless days, to become a whodunit, a mystery without obvious solution. Detectives are always tempted to swear by the 'most walkthrough' resolution of a case in order to avoid the work and grief that a whodunit will accrue over an extended period of time. But the truly forensic detectives—the ones committed to revelation rather than expedient conviction—will always slow the urge for the walkthrough, thereby keeping the case open for more inquisitive beats than the speedsters approve. These detectives are the whodunit guys, and they can be a pain in the neck. But everyone knows they are important.

It is similar when archival material is used as evidence for sociological or psychological interpretation. You have to resist fitting the evidence to prepared theories and received wisdom. Indeed, it is best to 'mooch' awhile with the evidence and stay as open as possible about it for as long as possible, keeping yourself ready to bamboozle common sense. You need to be hungry for endlessness at least as much as for the closure of conviction. Otherwise, how do you ever come to know anything more than just what you are already presuming and prescribing?

Every investigation needs a breadth of intuition, which is the pattern-seeking faculty that can supply the not-so-obvious connections that might account for the mystery at the root of the inquest. And to the extent that archives are stores of evidence rescued from oblivion, we need them to serve our pattern-seeking processes whenever we investigate what has happened in the past. In other words, we need our archives to be restless, active, protean and promiscuous whilst also being rigorous. Our archives have to spur speculation as much as they need to pin down verification.

Animus

Of course digital technology, with its tireless capacity for loss-less duplication, joining and layering, is bringing us closer to this good volatility, closer to the quickness that Vannevar Bush described in his extraordinarily prescient call for machines and institutions that behave 'as we may think', that mimic us and provoke us while they inform us.

This quickness, this animated vivacity is the secret of rousing knowledge. To illustrate, here is a parable. Early in *Running Dog*, Don DeLillo's acerbic fiction about collectors hustling for a fabled strip of pornographic film purportedly starring Adolph Hitler, a particularly ardent character observes: '[A] thing isn't fully erotic unless it has the capacity to move'. These days, the collector explains, everyone hankers for the shimmer that kinetics give. Capture this pulsating energy, and contemporary life succumbs to you because you have caught the animus of a world always on the make.[2]

If we remediate DeLillo's sentence, substituting 'an archive' for 'a thing' and dropping in 'generative' where 'erotic' used to sit, then my thesis is complete: an archive isn't fully generative unless it has the capacity to move. The joy of learning—the 'jouissance' of acknowledgement—comes when you can generate fresh understanding by shifting the semantic field within and around the key elements of a scene, helping the knowledge that is nested in the scene to bloom with an urge that is intensified by investigation. The energy of acknowledgement is indeed kinetic. To learn is to be *moved* so that, chastely expressed, an effective archive activates and arouses. A digital archive, because its components can be conjoined and then redistributed endlessly, has the capacity instantaneously and experimentally to integrate isolated elements so that an investigator can observe what comes of the association of this with that. Then in the next moment, one can try other semantic or aesthetic dalliances, and yet others again, all to see what gives a frisson, to see what is conceiveable when factors get united. Erotics yet again!

In this way a good archive is somewhat like DeLillo's libidinous version of cinema. But a good archive is also more than cinematic. For with cinema, once a full array of montages (think of them as audiovisual liaisons) have been tested in the editing room, the dalliances are locked off in a final version. After a certain point, with cinema, the speculations stop and the last proposition is set. But with the relational logic and the loss-less duplication afforded by digitised archives, the questing promiscuity of an avid investigator is potentially eternal. The archive can be made to behave like thought, like fantasy, consorting with new associative options constantly; the digital archive can stimulate the conjugal hunger of the speculator, setting the scene for the libidinous kick or twitch that sometimes pulses when revelation enriches realisation. (Note: the special affordances of digital archives are analysed in detail in *Changescapes*, the companion-piece to *Memoryscopes*.)

Tame the more louche connotations in the word 'lust', and you get close to how exciting a good digitised archive might be: an actively associative archive can encourage a lusty quest for knowledge. A digitised archive can generate understanding so that some new, possible world gets concocted in one's cognition when archived artefacts serving remembrance are arrayed for your speculation, when you can seek telling patterns amongst the dispersed but 'promiscuous' evidence that has been made ready for quick union, made ready by digitised copying, by catalogue-tagging, by metadata and the overall governance of relational coding. Or, to borrow the language that Stéphane Mallarmé used when he was explaining the thinking of the symbolist poets, an archive-user might proceed from this premise: '[because] objects are already in existence, it is not necessary to create them…all we have to do is grasp the relationships among them.'[3] Such associative moves do not lead to the prosaic procedures of a walkthrough; rather, they give urgency to the thriller that is a good whodunit driven by a poetic quest for knowledge.

The readiness to associate artefacts and information freely defines digital store-and-search systems. This endless ability to conjoin things can be compelling simply because it connects investigators—cast as voyeurs and fantasist speculators—to the animated world, granting them a dalliance with the past. But most importantly, with the combinative capacities of digital archives, investigators experience how *relationships amongst facts*, rather than just the facts or artefacts themselves, give deep insight. From this comprehensiveness, a chain of comprehension can unfurl. The first link is the glimmer of *sense* that arises from seeing the most pertinent points of relation amongst the cardinal integers in the documented world. Then a burgeoning *understanding* comes from grasping the cogency of those points that are well known already, linking them with those that are in danger of being forgotten, and conjoining them to fresh revelations that have been made possible in the shifting contexts afforded by the active archive. *Knowledge* grows then from tracing the filigree of relationships that subtend the full cache of recorded experience, past and present.

Such are the arguments and aspirations expressed in abstract, as I ponder how sense and understanding can intensify with a digital archive to make knowledge for a questing individual or for an entire culture. Now, to give these large notions more solid grounding, I bring a concrete example: a case study of an archive that I have been animating computationally over the past twenty years.

Life After Wartime

In the attic of the Justice and Police Museum (JPM) near Circular Quay in Sydney, there is a trove of 130,000 photographic negatives shot by police officers between the late 1890s and the early 1970s. The images were born of cruelty, desire, stupidity, bad luck, rage, greed and laziness, plus everyday political and economic pressures, all upwelling in an ocean town that was founded on much the same mess of impulses two centuries ago when criminal and military cultures from Britain piled in on top of the local Indigenous world.

The Pulse in the Past

So the JPM archive registers patterns that have long shaped the town. Mostly the negatives show the mid-twentieth-century version of Sydney, featuring the cars, trams and electrical implements as well as the guns, cudgels and liquor bottles that have accompanied malfeasance and misadventure here through the decades. The images are filed in thousands of boxes containing manila envelopes. Usually some india-ink code has been daubed on the side to indicate that the box holds a spatter of cases relating to a particular month of a particular year. Each envelope, batching between three and thirty negatives, encompasses a single investigation. On the front of the envelope, a photographer-detective has written his name, the date, a location and a terse summary of what is being documented: 'Break Enter Steal', 'Loiter in Yard, 'Consorting with Menace'.

And that is all. That is the full extent of the interpretive clues offered by the JPM archive. There is no comprehensive catalogue. No investigators' notebooks, no charge-sheets, judgements or appended newspaper clippings. If the metadata ever existed, it has all gone missing over the years, most likely when the pictures were rescued from rising floodwaters in a warehouse in the inner-west of Sydney during the 1980s. Nothing *conclusive* remains. There are no authoritative decrees that put an end to the narratives that each tersely tagged image stimulates in the imagination of its appreciator. Comprising a jumbled almanac of a brusque city, the negatives provoke, attract and disturb while they educate. But they never resolve with any note of certainty.

For me these images offer something richer than certainty: they prompt endless questions and unsettling accounts concerning real lives and places that have been pressed as luminous energy on to photographic film. For me the archive keens and yelps. Sometimes it moans. Other times it gasps. And curses. And dissembles. The negatives portray the town in a pained and piquant way that contradicts but also complements the shiny impressions of pleasure that radiate from Sydney's advertising industry and popular magazines. When I mull over the archive, I understand the liveliness of the town better because the pictures thrum with mendacity and mortality, helping me see the historical and cosmic forces that swell sombre beneath the shimmers of the gorgeous town. 'And this also…has been one of the dark places of the earth'. Thus wrote Joseph Conrad at the start of *Heart of Darkness*. He was describing London. The JPM archive gives a sense of how Conrad's decree can also be applied to Sydney.

Here is a typical day for me in the archive, riffling through the envelopes. With my mind concentrated by the words on the file (for example, 'Suicide with Gelignite—Redfern Park Toilet Block'), I imagine what I am about to confront. The anticipation builds while my gloved fingers pinch at the edges of an acetate sheet that I raise for a squinted preview before resting it on the lightbox, where I will be able to dwell in the image until the anticipation either fizzles or ignites. I might see banality: some scrappy tract of lawn scarred and scorched in an aftermath; a staved-in old shed that has to smell acrid; or a brown bottle up-ended in a scuffed army boot. Often I cannot comprehend anything till I translate the contrasts of the image, inverting the obscurities from negative to positive so an illuminated world can emerge, obeying the retinal logic that my mind's eye has learned to expect. Then, from time to time, I see something that burns my senses and stops me thinking. And all the while, I go diving every which way through a thousand surges of narration, wondering: 'What about *this story* as a way to account for this picture I'm seeing?'

In the JPM archive, the pictured streets and rooms, the people and their associated objects all seem to be in a state of shock.

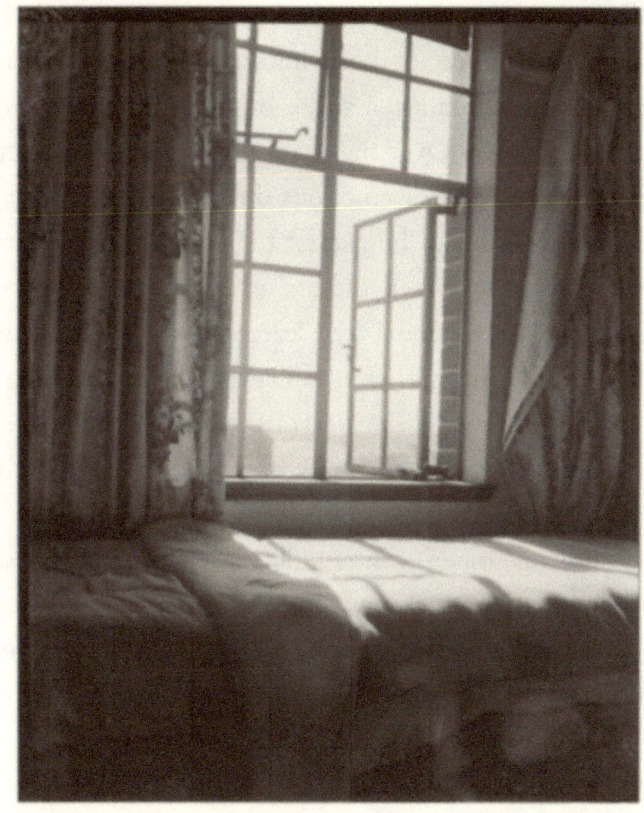

```
Autumn will come soon.
Cooling in stealth.
Delivered slyly down in dull waiting dusk.
```
           Suspicious Death, Kings Cross, 1954. FP08_0068_004.

Life After Wartime *archive, still with*
three breath-texts stuck to it
and sounds swirling around it.

Referring to a different but related context Luc Sante has given an apt description of a box of New York City police pictures that he found: they were 'like the voice print of a scream'.[4] This is almost right for the JPM pictures. But to be precise, they don't scream so much as they flare. As I hold them to the light, they ignite like a struck match and then glare for a moment before dimming down either to sharp luminance or dull banality. I sense something scorching, a surge of anxious electrical qualm plus a glandular scald. Over the years I have come to understand that this is a symphony of emotions directly associated with the evidence, and it needs to be part of the accounts that I facilitate with the photographs when the archive is activated for making sense leading to knowledge. I have learned that the flare ignites on the surface of the image, then it radiates not only across to other images but also through the nervous system of everyone who looks at it until it gets parcelled interpretively, or is refused, in the viewer's cerebration.

This intermission—between flaring emotion and cooling intellection—is where the power lurks in the JPM pictures. It is a power that an archival configuration of the pictures needs to heed and harness when contextual information gets nested around the images. It is the power that has guided an experimental, digital configuration of a selected portion of the JPM collection—a configuration that is a computer-based archive in the form of a story-engine called *Life After Wartime* (*LAW*)—that I have worked with collaborators to compose after we have digitised about 1500 of the JPM images at the same time as we have tagged hundreds of dedicated sounds and thousands of texts that 'attract' to each pictorial file. (See: www.lifeafterwartime.com.) With the coded and combinative design of this *LAW* archive—this digital subset of the old JPM archive—we have programmed each image to combine with a select batch of others and with the metadata of the overall system so the *LAW* 'engine' can produce pulsed utterances (they are not always sentences) associated with the pictures: utterances that activate an outbursting little surge of thought-and-emotion that can be said in a breath and apprehended in a blink. The pulse comes from allowing the convergence (where image, text and sound combine) to be followed by a divergence (where the image, text and sound all go back to their respective databased repositories) to be followed by the next code-governed convergences that

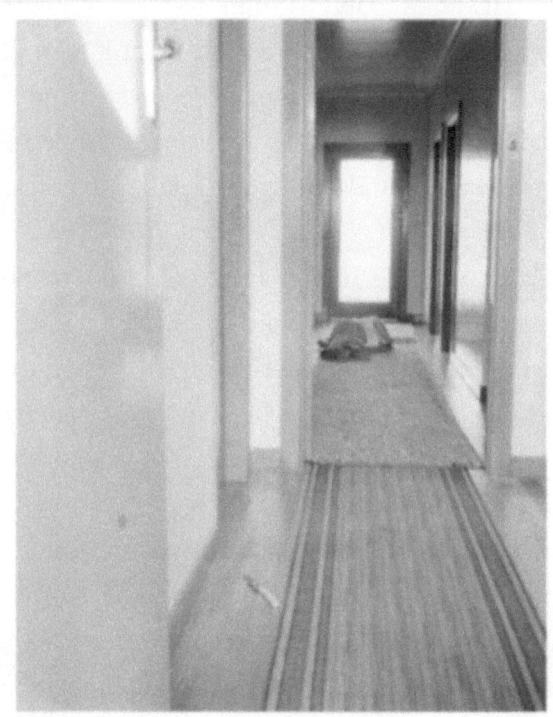

Life After Wartime *archive, still with
three breath-texts stuck to it
and sounds swirling around it.*

manifest as thoughtful speculations and as aesthetic combinations of sound, image and text, all making a rhythm that is simultaneously narrative, painterly and musical.

The idea is that by activating the associative logic of *LAW*, viewers get to sense the import of each pulsed utterance in their nervy bodies. As the photograph flares in front of your eyes while also offering text and a sound-composition about it, you perceive myriad options arrayed within each image, you catch and marshal your breath, and then you gather the words into skeined lines of interpretation while the sounds pull your feelings in around your thinking.

Crucially, it is a *palpable* line of interpretation, composed in a form that is entire and organic: words utterable in a full, single breath that is quickened by the flickering of picture and the flight of the sounds. Once supplied, the words and sounds draw something out from the picture; something you assay in your breathing, sentient self. Then as time keeps pulsing, the process reiterates and more propositions wax and then wane. The interpretations generated thus are profligate, unending. The opposite of the stilled storage of interpretion that conclusive accounting targets when a doubtless historian seeks eternal verities. The digital archive can be more dubious, generative and ontologically generous than that.

Endlessness—a conclusion

So it goes with the *LAW* version of the JPM archive. Digitised images, sounds and words interweave to make a world of interpretation applicable to Sydney circa 1950. Every picture in the *LAW* archive is a whodunit. And the accruing interpretations are myriad. Not fanciful. Not irresponsible. But restless, legion, fugitive and contestable depending on the context clustering around each moment of interpretation.

Let's reprise some of the questions I posed at the start of this chapter:

- How can archives be truly moving?
- How can they be used not as repositories but as stimulant events?
- How might they exercise the motile, relational systems of memory, instead of just freezing and storing its miscellaneous componentry?

My hope is that the particular experience of composing the *LAW* archive offers some answers in general. The force of artefacts comes in their association, not in their singularity. *LAW* offers a dynamic, interactive and inquisitive system that strums memory and desire and encourages us to do as we may feel and as we may think (borrowing Vannevar Bush's language one more time).

For its full force to be well comprehended, every artefact in an archive needs its others. Every artefact needs to be altered in its contextualisations and composite reanimations as it gets associated with different but pertinent files. This way, the archive is replete with possible worlds of speculation and imagination built from the records. Memory gets activated in the service of imagination, which is in turn subjected to the rigours of analysis and evaluation. With an active archive, in truth, conclusiveness is the least compelling affordance in the system. More importantly, the processes of fabulation-and-inquisition should go on without stint. There tends to be no pulse with conclusiveness. The coldest case of all is the one that seems completely uncontroversial and settled. Lifeless. Active, digitally recombinative archives keep every case warm, ready to be disturbed and realigned and re-investigated.

And this is a good thing, I contend. For all the meanings and feelings of the world are ours and they are therefore always needing contention, requiring new fabulation, evincing fresh ardour and demanding endless verification. With digital systems our archives can shadow and shiver the world. Our archives do not have to still the world down. The past is more lively than that and deserves better.

Notes
1   W. Sanders, *Detective Work: a study of criminal investigations*, Free Press, New York, 1977, p. 174.
2   D. DeLillo, *Running Dog*, Knopf, New York, 1978, p. 15.
3   Y. Seishi, *The Essence of Modern Haiku*, Mangajin, Atlanta, 1993, p. xix.
4   L. Sante, *Evidence*, Farrar, Strauss and Giroux, New York, 1992, p. 60.

8

AESTHETICS AND SOMETHING MORE THAN MEANING IN FORENSIC PHOTOGRAPHIC EVIDENCE

In chapter seven ('The Pulse in the Past') of this book, I described the police photography archive of the Justice and Police Museum (JPM) in Sydney. In that chapter I considered how the archive can be activated by digital systems so that the viewer gets *to think* with the associative plenitude of the thousands of images that ghost the everyday history of twentieth-century Sydney. Now, in this chapter, I want to concentrate on how *feeling* works in tandem with thinking when you respond to the pictures held by all the cursorily inscribed envelopes jumbled in the JPM archive.

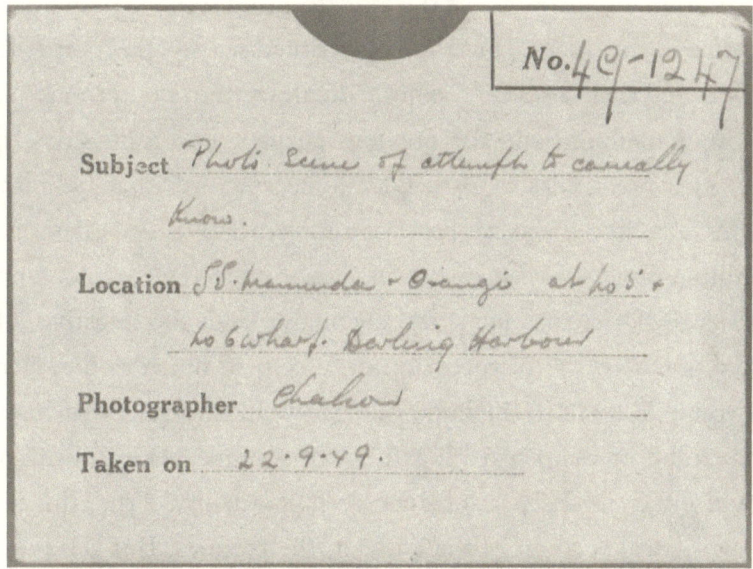

JPM Case File Envelope: 'Photo Scenes of attempt to carnally Know'

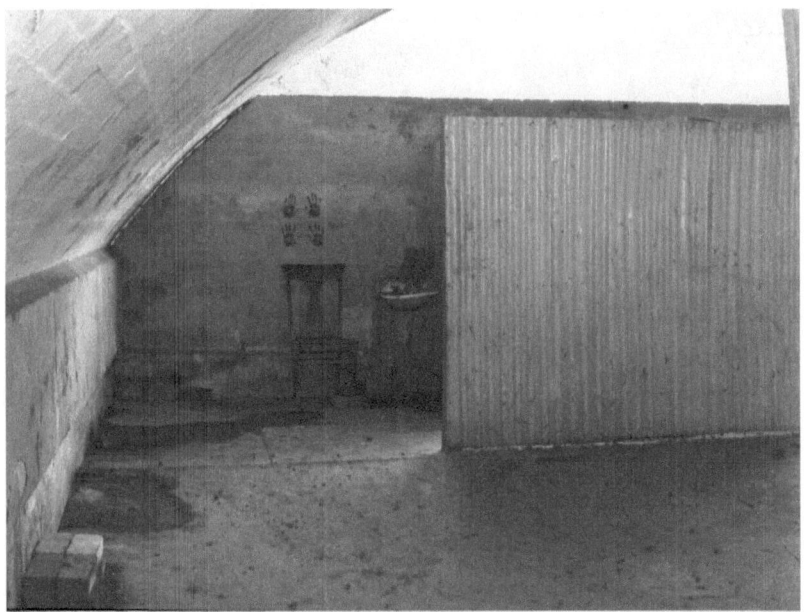

'Grievous Bodily Harm', Glebe, 1956, FP_008_0113_002

My starting point is to note how the JPM photographs carry an *excessive* impact. Admittedly the viewer is primed, by the envelope notes and by the context of the attic, to bring some melodramatic animus to the images, but the documented streets and rooms, the people and their associated objects do all seem to be in shock.

As I mentioned in the previous chapter, Luc Sante's description of a box of New York City police pictures that he found seems apt: 'like the voice print of a scream.'[1] But Sante describes the lingering *after-effect* of the images. In the JPM photographs, one gets the scream *during* the encounter with the negative. Or, more precisely, the pictures do not scream so much as they flare. As you hold them to the light, they ignite like a struck match and then some of them glare hurtfully for a while before dimming down either to sharp luminance or dull banality. True, this is a metaphorical account of the affect in the pictures. But it is literal too, insofar as the viewer does feel the effects of the flare: holding an image at arms length, as if to insulate its charge, one often senses the image causing a burning surge of anxious electical qualm within oneself. Effectively, affectively, *aesthetically*, the flare ignites on the surface of the image, then it radiates through your nervous system till it gets parcelled interpretively (or is refused) in your cerebration.

Which brings us to the fact that these images hold some *aesthetic* force that is materially present and cannot be overlooked when we try to use the photographs for knowing something about the world that they somehow ghost and serve. I take 'aesthetic' to be concerned not with evaluations of beauty or assertions of taste. Instead, it is tied to the etymology that brought the word from its origins in Classical Greek, via the German language, into English late in the eighteenth century: '*aisthetikos*: perceptible by the senses'.[2] In an aesthetic encounter, therefore, the senses are engaged, such that your sensibility is stalled and supplemented so that a new draft of sensemaking is required. An aesthetic experience takes the appreciator palpably through his or her senses toward the intellection of fresh sense, toward a new comprehension that will cohere after thoughtful work is done in response to the feelings that have welled up during the intensified perception. And because there are aesthetic factors in any material evidence insofar as the traces of any event or object are perceptible by the senses, then our most comprehensive interpretations of that evidence must take active account of all the sensory stimuli as well as the cerebral syntheses associated with it. To miss the aesthetic components is to miss a good part of the valency in the material, to miss some access to the world that whelped the evidence.

Japanese aesthetic traditions are germane here. Haiku writers, for example, attend to a moving configuration of perceptions—a glimpse of colour, let's say, plus a special tincture or texture

combined with a peculiar sound pressing through a moment—
that can resonate in the reader's sensibility so that, as I have already
quoted Thomas Hoover evoking so lucidly, 'the mind is struck as
with a hammer, bringing the senses up short and releasing a flood
of associations'. Here is an example from Ranko, an eighteenth-
century master:

> Waves of heat;
> At each stroke of the hoe—
> How the earth smells.[3]

Once the multiple senses have been piqued in the encounter with
the select fragments offered by the haiku, the reader strains for a
reverberant insight, knowing it will wane in the same instant it is
grasped. Thus as R. H. Blyth explains, the objective of the haiku
writer is to cause a 'temporary enlightenment in which we see
into the life of things'.[4]

Might 'the life of things' be another way of saying 'material
culture'? Perhaps the life of things is what an anthropologist or
a museum visitor strives to know. Certainly it is what police
detectives seek—the life of things—when they go gathering scin-
tillas of possible insights for priming speculative accounts that get
tested first in their own minds and then later in the forum of the
lawcourt, tested against plausibilities determined by human nature,
by moral and ethical strictures and by the laws of chemistry and
physics as well as the laws of the land. From this profusion of
initial accounts, a viable case can get sifted into existence. So,
starting with a world blown open, the detectives drive to shut it
down, to bring doubtless judgement.

But the most dedicated investigators know it is best not
to settle too quickly on a conclusive hypothesis, even though

Aesthetics and Something More than Meaning

everyone nearby the crime hankers after closure. As explained in the previous chapter, William Sanders noticed in his great book, *Detective Work*, that police tend to assume there are two kinds of crimes: walkthroughs and whodunits. And the truly forensic detectives—the ones committed to revelation rather than expedient conviction—will always slow the urge for the walkthrough, thereby keeping the case open for just a few inquisitive beats longer than the speedsters approve.

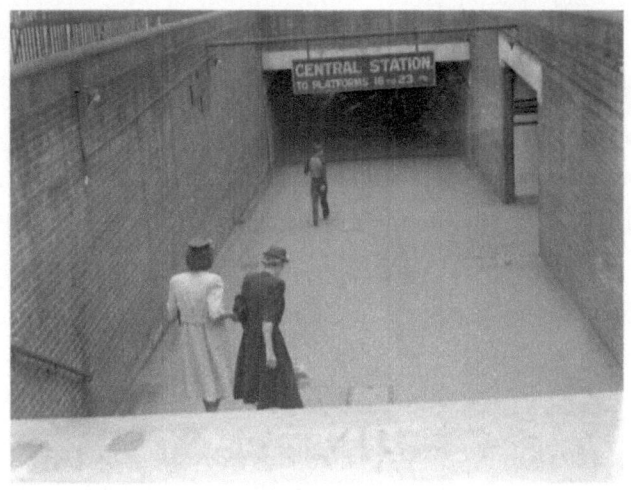

Walking is just a struggle with falling.

Somebody's hissing: "Do you want me to explain to them how come we're together?"

What makes it move like that, the thing in the shadows?

Death by Fall, Surry Hills, 1948.   FP08_166_003

The process can go similarly when material culture is used as evidence for interpretation. You have to resist fitting the evidence to prepared theories. You need a hunger for endlessness at least as much as for closure or conclusivenss. Otherwise, how does one ever come to know anything more than just what is presumed and prescribed?

And so it is, I know, with the JPM photographs. Every case is a whodunnit. And the interpretations are myriad. Indeed they might even be endless. For the cues on the envelopes get you started, and then your sense of the city plus your knowledge of the times plus your feelings about human nature and 'the life of things' all guide you along. But nothing stops the speculation with these photographs.

This is where digital systems can keep thoughts and feelings active and *applied* when speculations get roused by the JPM evidence. Indeed, the activation goes both ways, for the JPM collection also helps us investigate how digital systems can shape and be shaped to contemporary sense and sensibility, given that digital systems are designed to keep interpretation open and evolving.

To press this point, I need to pause now and present a brief history of cultural forms, starting with the emergence of the novel, then considering cinema, and ending with an analysis of digital databases. (Full disclosure: some of these ideas are also presented—in a different context for different discursive purposes—in *Changescapes*, the companion-piece to *Memoryscopes*.)

In 1957 Ian Watt published *The Rise of the Novel*, which examined 'the enduring connexions between the distinctive literary qualities of the novel and those of the society in which it began and flourished'.[5] This society—eighteenth-century western Europe—had become complicated. With the waning of the Church and the discrediting of the notion of the divine rights of kings, most European states were experiencing the rise of mercantilism motivated by an ascendant new class, the bourgeoisie.

Aesthetics and Something More than Meaning

Commoners began to imagine that they might take charge of their own destiny. All this seemed unprecedented, novel.

So a speculative form developed that helped readers consider the effects of free-willed action. With a novel in hand and a plot in mind, readers could establish a scene that was really felt although not entirely real, where they could pose orienting questions. For instance:

> If a character acted in *this* particular manner, what repercussions might flow from the assertion of his or her new freedoms?

or...

> Within *these* particular settings, what are the determining factors—such as the desires and fears of the portrayed characters, such as the systems of affordance and impedance in the represented society, such as the workings of nature or fate—what are the determining factors most likely to press upon a self-assertive citizen?

Watt started from the premise that artistic forms tend to mimic the psychological, social and political conditions prevalent in the particular era that gives rise to them. He contended that early novelists such as Daniel Defoe and Henry Fielding developed literary techniques for dramatising the realisation of bourgeois individuals. The novels tested the lineaments of their characters' private sensibilities, how these characters might create opportunities for themselves, how they might conduct self-reflective interior monologues with which to forge new, negotiable relationships between the self and the world. Watt showed how writers invented textual conventions by sketching settings and evoking the innermost thought-flows and mood-swings of protagonists performing in imagined narrative worlds which readers could compare to their own, lived worlds. And he showed how these characters came to stand in and speak for readers who were trying to grasp the intricacies of living amidst proliferating new details and increased secular opportunities and responsibilities.

The way novelistic characters worked on and in the reader, this was experimental and speculative rather than traditional or didactic. Different from the allegory and the religious parable, which are part of oral custom and which reinforce established moral codes, the novel arose to facilitate ethical innovation and to test possibly outdated moral impositions, to help readers scrutinise the intellectual and emotional conundrums in an altering political domain. Thus the novel was a new technology for examining psychic models of a possible personality. Referring to such models and matching them against received knowledge of lived experience, readers could measure options for themselves. Here was a cultural form that empowered people to reflect on all the novelty that defined their changeful times. No wonder it was suddenly popular. It was needed. And it was shaped by and for the contemporary culture.

Watt showed that when a new form of art or a popular mode of communication arises and takes hold, it reflects changes that have recently occurred or are presently occurring in psychology and society. Invented and adopted at exactly the time it is needed, a new popular form causes change while paradoxically reflecting how change has already commenced.

Indeed, through this very process, the novel would eventually be superseded (which is not to say eliminated) by a newly predominant form of narrative modelling—cinema—which emerged at a time when individual psychologies and social configurations were changing yet again, this time under the pressure of the modern world's kinetics. In other words, cinema was developed for enhancing peoples' understanding of the sensory 'attack' that assailed every individual psyche once the speedy, mechanical modes of transport, communication and commodity production became widespread during the Industrial Revolution. With the machine age and with the resultant urban expansions at the end of the nineteenth century, the modern world was being redefined by the way energy was expressed in urgent, mechanical rhythms. And cinema tracked this shift in impetus. Cinema was consumed avidly worldwide right from the outset because, with its percussive assemblages of nervous stimuli, it was synchronised to the contemporary psyche and the contemporary social and physical environment. Keenly attuned to each viewer's sensorium within the urban-industrial tumult, cinema was the aesthetic form arising from the modern metropolis.

When cinema loomed all around the world, new nations and social masses were forming, wondering how to fuse several scattered constituencies into new, singular states. Thus in conjunction with other distance-devouring technologies—especially the railroad and the telegraph—cinema helped individuals and communities imagine unified new worlds gathered in a feasible spatio-temporal frame where previously there had been only estranged and disconnected populations clustered in locations that had been unable to synchronise across great administrative time lags. With the advent of cinema, audiences could envisage associations with far-flung people and places all meshing in 'organic' rhythms as fast as heartbeats and almost as quick as thought. The movies projected lively protagonists in a welter of social scenarios. Thus with the aid of cinema, a new nation—a new social, spatio-temporal amalgam—could be envisaged where once it had been unimaginable. Film editors deployed the principle of montage to federate new states of possibility. For the crowds assembled in the smoky theatres, seeing these new states could lead to believing in the nation.

This happened in Japan, Russia, France, Britain, the USA and Australia, to name just the obvious cases. Consider Australia in the 1910s, in the inaugural years of the Federal Government: cinema enabled people in Gympie, Sydney and Adelaide, let's say, to share a perceptual and a conceptual frame where they had previously been dissociated. An associative imagination was fostered nationwide. Civic reality and cinematic possibility: each impelled the other. A nation could be construed as a new federation, and this new order could be imagined in place of the squabbling states and hamlets that had previously been misaligned in geographical and ideological alienation.

But cinema has its limits. A definitive characteristic of the movies is the way they 'lock off' their several dynamic parts into a final version: the 'release print'. This ultimate inflexibility of cinema is similar to the way most national-scale communities responded to the turbulence of modernity by insisting that their societies first synchronise energetically to the machine world and then stabilise permanently once the new political state was realised. With its production regimens always driving toward 'lock off' cinema is a conservative form, like nationalism. Cinema and nationalism: each serves a popular, paradoxical desire for the simultaneous acknowledgement and cessation of change. Indeed, this is one of the traits we love about cinema: it shows the thrill of energetic convergence and world-creation at the same time as it proposes an eventual end to flux and uncertainty. With a film, the final edit is a stable state, a kingdom of kinetic excitement with a reassuring climate of completion.

Comparing the nexus of cinema and nationalism with the contemporary dyad of digital media and globalisation, one can ask whether multimedia databases have arisen to reflect and impel our contemporary psychic and social conditions. Like cinema, digital multimedia can federate disparate elements (sounds, texts, graphics, perspectives, vistas and audio-visual rhythms) into astonishing new configurations. These similarities prompted Lev Manovich to create a genesis myth about multimedia being first created literally out of cinematic material, out of old film stock stippled with data-entry punctures in the 'digital computer' that Konrad Zuse constructed in 1936.[6]

But unlike cinema (and unlike nationalism), digital multimedia databases produce syntheses that are explicitly provisional. (In this respect they are like globalisation.) Because of the dynamics of its file structures and the integrating, evolving codes that get applied to those files, any digital multimedia configuration is a contentious event in a continuous process rather than a completed, content-full object; it is always ready to be dismantled and reassembled into new alignments as soon as the constituent files have been federated in response to momentarily prevailing 'world conditions'. Moreover, the constituent files can alter as new data are absorbed and old or 'junk' data are 'trashed'.

In other words, because a multimedia database rarely gets 'locked-off', its component elements can always be pulled apart, sent back to their file-caches, ready to be re-arranged into newly iterated federations. (In this respect it is like our unstable contemporary lives, so buffeted with ever-altering values, opportunities, anxieties and obligations all ingressing, egressing and upwelling,

Memoryscopes

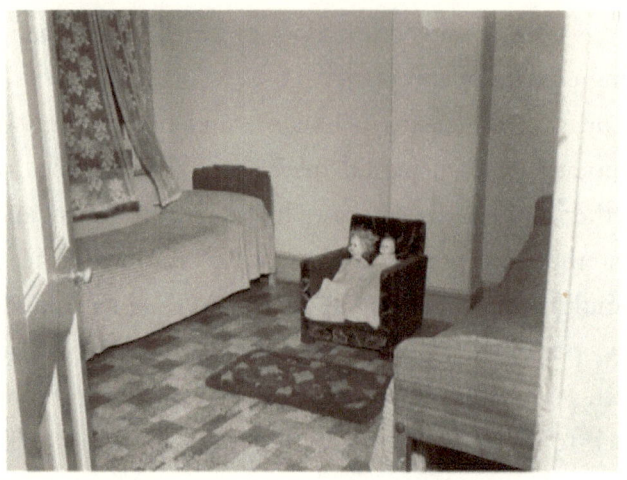

```
For five or six minutes the room is
breathless and the air is metallic on the
tongue.

Every live thing lingers frozen, unblinking.

Then the city understands and tries to bring
comfort in.
```

Marrickville, Grievous Bodily Harm, 1955. FP08_0109_002.

in part, because of globalisation, migration and multi-culturalism.) By dramatising divergence and dispersion as well as convergence, a digital multimedia system can react to variant stimuli from the environment or from its investigative participants (who are part of the environment, of course). Taking some of their dynamics from the channel-switching, overlaying montage-effects that radio and television have always afforded, digital multimedia systems can re-conform themselves restlessly in ways that a cinema print or a novel or a written historical account is not designed to do. Such digital multimedia systems can reflect and impel how we live now in relational engagement within myriad influences that are dynamically networked in constantly evolving conditions of accessibility via stored, searchable information. Already these contingent systems have become so much a part of everyday life that it is difficult to construe how radically they have altered our attitudes to the local, the remote, the immediate, the reverberant.

It should be obvious by now why the digital database is an amenable form for working with the endlessly interpretable JPM images. But short of booting up a nearby computer, there is still some work to do for the JPM database here in text.

When writing about writing, one can quote an exemplary section of text and analyse it, in text, as text. By contrast, with a multimedia database, the commentator must evoke the exemplar in the alien medium of verbiage, before using those stolid words to analyse the system's non-verbal affordances and mutability. Similar issues of 'ekphrastic' translation confront the cinema critic, of course. But at least cinema now has a lexicon of tropes and a canon of 'classics' that can be nominated so readers and writers all know somewhat the thing they have gathered around. Because the digital multimedia database is such a new cultural form, there are few canonical references yet, and it is still difficult to have confidence that everyone knows the cited examples. This is the context in which I must now describe the 'dramatic database', known as *Life After Wartime—(LAW)* story engine, that I have developed from the JPM photographs, collaborating with a team of producers and designers in order to highlight and investigate the restless meanings and fugitive feelings that proliferate in the pictures.[7]

Because of the 'aftermath qualities' of the JPM photographs, one feels an urge to proffer stories to account for them, to say what characters have acted and what events have occurred to make the scenes appear the way they do. But because of the dearth of accompanying information—given that almost all the metadata relating to the photographs have gone missing—one must accept that all accounts of the pictures will be speculative, no matter how well informed one might be, historically, about the town and the times that produced the scenes.

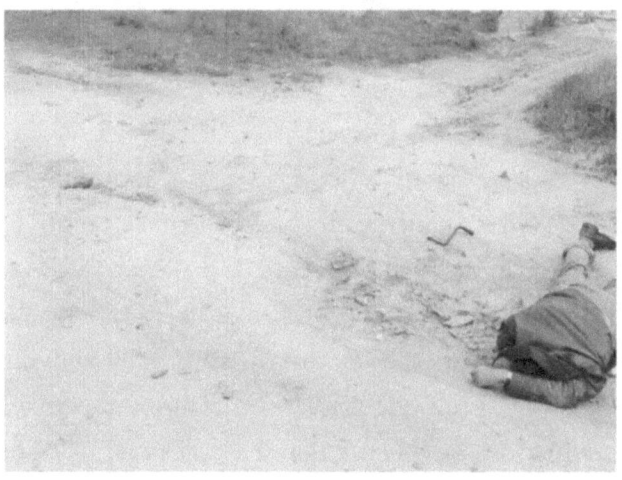

```
A mutilated car is struggling down a dirt
track.

Time blows like a starburst and just hangs
in the air.

Every thing gets bent where it wants to go
straight.
```

Avalon, Murder, 1956. FP09_0076_008.

After several years testing how best to use the images in a street history of Sydney, the *LAW* team has composed a responsive sound+image device that mimics and further stimulates the dramatic disturbance that plays in your consciousness when you encounter the photographs. This speculative engine combines three reservoirs of file-types—images, caption-texts and music+sound components—all governed by relational attractions

Aesthetics and Something More than Meaning

and repulsions that have been designed into the governing code of the system. This code determines the attractions and repulsions of image to image, image to text, text to sound, sound to image, and so on. The code activates the aesthetic characteristic of the pulses and the flares that are the defining 'forces' in the pictures. Depending on which particular images the investigator chooses while *LAW* is throwing batches of pictures forward in turbulent patterns, the system gains cohesion according to the history of each investigator's interaction with the database.

Over time, there gather thousands of somewhat runic micro-narratives plus a suite of mood-modulations (delivered in music, sound patterns and rhythms of activeness), until a debatable meta-narrative world gains critical mass, so that the entire image-world of the archive is steeped with a kind of creeping, historicised fabulation. Crucially, each investigator will gather up a different set of micro-narratives and moods and each investigator will tend toward a larger story in idiosyncratic and personally stamped ways. Moreover, each investigator will encounter qualities of themselves as well as qualities of the archive. In part, it is yourself you find when you delve into *LAW*. But it is yourself in relation to real patterned evidence shaped by a real patterned world. (For a general account of the various iterations of the *LAW* project, see www.lifeafterwartime.com.)

Engaging with *LAW*, you deduce soon enough that you are not just a reader or a receiver of this historicist artwork. Rather you are implicated as an investigator and as a kind of 'quarry' also, as the system begins to 'follow' you obliquely, offering aspects of itself in response to the types of inquiries you have already made of the database. As you figure 'what if' propositions, trying out postulative relations between various elements and observing how those relationships play out, you assess how productive of sense or fascination your speculations seem to be while *LAW* offers germs of stories that you both doubt and appreciate. With this sceptical yet postulative attitude, you wonder about the world that is witnessed in the pictures. You consider what might have happened. And you test those considerations against the contextually established knowledge that you have already assembled. In other words, you wonder and worry away at what you presently feel to be true for those scenes. Interpretations get aligned with commonsense beliefs, with what is already agreed to have happened in the represented world and with what the *LAW* system keeps proffering as possible interpretations. Again and again, without rest, you must speculate and test. You are never receiving one unarguable line of interpretation. Although you sense interpretive patterns and narrative lines emerging and evolving, conclusiveness does not beckon. Rather, a dramatic hypothesis blooms that is always offering many different foci and perspectives even as each investigator pursues several particular trajectories of inquiry.

Speculate and test. Essay and assay. *LAW* is meant to encourage this forensic rhythm in the imagination and the intellect. It prompts a kind of divination. It is just one example of 'digital systems art'. I think of it as an historical and aesthetic ecology defined by actions contending with reactions, animated by individual assertion contending with systematic resistance and adjustment.

Throughout *Of Two Minds*, a study of hypertext, Michael Joyce examines how this new, interactive mode of writing and reading prioritises *structural* thought over *serial* thought.[8] As I noted in an earlier chapter, Joyce explains how the cross-referencing and branching allowed by hypertext have arisen to serve a readership that is really a forensic audience, an audience looking to take charge of their own convictions, looking to *construct and test* rather than to *receive and accept* their worldview. This is an investigative readership that knows there are many variabilities and volatilities defining life now; indeed there are so many such variabilities that it is implausible to rely on the reception of one conclusive line of argument or explanation (delivered in serial thought). This is because the premises on which any one serial discourse is founded are nowadays always debatable and subject to rapid redundancy. Instead, a contemporary investigative reader scans the field of lived and represented experience structurally, assaying the meanings and feelings prevailing in the dynamic complex of tendencies, mutations and options that constitute the life of the somewhat free-willed subject today.

More than just an informatic or technical tool, every multimedia database—even the most bureaucratic or functional ones that are seemingly devoid of poetics or aesthetics—is infused with aesthetics and semantics. Every multimedia database involves human–computer interaction and is therefore 'dramatic' and evolutionary somehow, because the interaction introduces novelty or change which challenges the established configurations of the system. Considered as an exemplary cultural form, the interactive multimedia database has a cultural history at the same time as it represents an innovative break with other representational forms such as the novel, the oil painting or the cinema feature. This cultural form has arisen to address the psychic and social dynamics of our times.

So, after several years analysing how to use the JPM images in a street history of Sydney, I have learned to acknowledge and emphasise the pulses in the pictures by composing a voluble sound+image device that mimics the dramatic disturbance that plays out when you encounter the photographs and you feel your senses sharpen to a pain or thrill or you sense yourself dulling

Memoryscopes

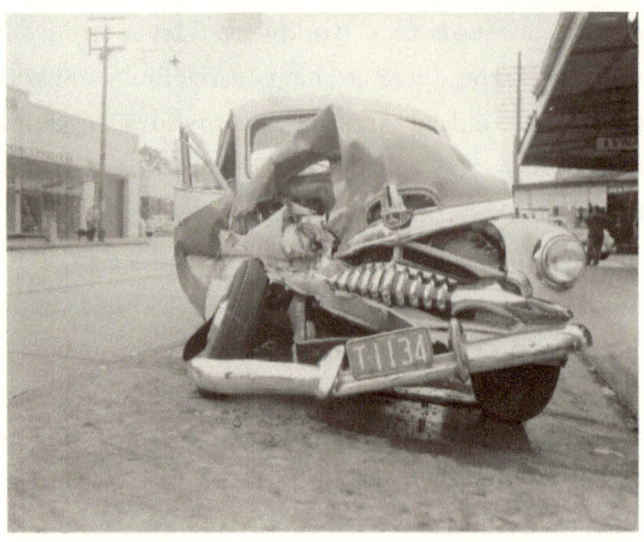

```
See how an object can take the shape of a
scream.

Understand that vim can ebb in a warm
sluice.

Accept that heat is just a brief sigh made
by cold.
```

Croydon, Motor Vehicle Accident, 1954. FP09_080_008.

down with an ache. I have learned how to help the viewer register the flare in these pictures and thereby experience some of the insights and emotions that wait in each case file. Of course, it is a subjective 'truth' that I conjure with *LAW*. I promote a felt knowledge that is evoked as in fiction, never proven by conventional standards of history; but it is also creditable as a testimony to some of the social, psychological and fateful forces that have animated the photographed city as the past has made the present.

Taking the notion of the pictorial flare seriously, the *LAW* team has developed a story-engine that continuously strikes little hammers in the mind so that an ever-developing concatenation of minor-key epiphanies can chime for viewers as they consider the ways to make sense of the seemingly depthless power in the photographs so that a flush of the special 'qualia' in the photographs can circulate and essay liaisons before disengaging to seek again freshly montaged ignitions that might light up portions of the city's lesser-known past.

Some cultures might feel pantheism, or perhaps the presence of ancestors in the JPM pictures. For me, the images give an historical yet personal pulse that is activated, then reactivated and also altered, over time, in the sparking gap between the picture and the viewer. Activated in the digital database that is *LAW*, this pulse causes a kind of sensory witnessing tempered by intellection, a process that is simultaneously palpable and dubious. It is a contentious pulse, a flaring experience that passes even as it emerges. This pulse prompts me to know my place aesthetically, to know it narratively, imaginatively and with a feeling of inner, nervous conviction that is matched by worry and scepticism. Such are the moods and rhythms of now.

Note: the images in this chapter all appear courtesy of the Justice and Police Museum, Sydney. They are part of *LAW* sub-project called *Accident Music*, which can be accessed at: http://blogs.hht.net.au/justice/index.php/category/accident-music/.

Notes

1. L. Sante, *Evidence*, Farrar, Strauss and Giroux, New York, 1992, p. 60.
2. G. A. Wilkes and W. A. Krebs (eds) *Collins English Dictionary*, 3rd edition, Harper Collins, Sydney, 1991, p. 24.
3. R. H. Blyth, *Haiku*, vol. II, Hokuseido Press, Tokyo, 1950, p. 77.
4. R. H. Blyth, *Haiku*, vol. I, Hokuseido Press, Tokyo, 1949, p. 270.
5. I. Watt, *The Rise of the Novel: studies in Defoe, Richardson and Fielding*,

Penguin, Harmondsworth, 1963, (first published Chatto & Windus, London, 1957.) p. 7.
6   L. Manovich, *The Language of New Media*, MIT Press, Cambridge, MA, 2001, p. 25.
7   The principal members of the LAW team, along with me as writer and director, are: Kate Richards, producer and artist; Greg White, programmer and sound designer; Aaron Seymour, graphic designer; and Chris Abrahams, musician and sound designer.
8   M. Joyce, *Of Two Minds: hypertext pedagogy and poetics*, University of Michigan Press, Ann Arbor, 1995.

9

SELF EXTRACTION

Spend a morning browsing the online archive of *The Paris Review*, sampling the extended conversations with established authors. You will learn how there as many creative manoeuvres as there are writers.[1] However, in this chapter I will examine just one authorial ruse. It is a method that I have investigated for a couple of decades: the process of concentrating on some highly resonant influence or extant text or object so as to translate the old thing into a new, personal utterance. I will draw on a classic essay by T. S. Eliot, plus some thoughts by the German philosopher and filmmaker Alexander Kluge, and a stray comment in Bob Dylan's memoir. Finally I will offer examples from my own creative practice to indicate how in the mutative process of translating a set of stimuli into a new expression, various ekphrastic and multimodal manoeuvres might be helpful for cajoling the work out of oneself.

So this essay prods a basic enigma: where do our utterances come from? How much memory, how much imagination in our expressions? In Australia we get to pursue this question across a vast expanse, from the epic reach of Indigenous knowledge-systems through to the intimate scale of lyrics, lullabies and prayers drawn from myriad immigrant cultures. But no matter what the context, every writer transmits from a matrix of what-has-gone-before. From a tradition.

In *Chronicles: volume one*, Bob Dylan reminisces about the months when, barely out of his teens in the early 1960s, he began hustling for gigs in New York City. Dossing in strange apartments stuffed with record collections, letting go of the Zimmerman family name that he never felt described him, listening to the non-stop verbiage of obsessive almanacers like Dave Van Ronk, Dylan discovered his creative self in the hubbub of the reprised songs that make the American folk repertoire:

> I could make things up on the spot all based on folk music structure…You could write twenty or more songs off…one melody by slightly altering it…I could slip in verses or lines from old spirituals or blues. There was little headwork involved. What I usually did was start out with something, some kind of line written in stone and then turn it with another line—make it add up to something else than it originally did.[2]

Thus Dylan might start exploring a Blind Willie McTell blues song on a Monday. By Friday, five hundred renditions later, the song had mutated—in riffs and rhymes—into something as new as it was old, as Dylan kinked a line here, changed a verb there, bent a stray melody around a 'wrong' run of similes and lost McTell while being guided by him. This was nothing mystical. It was the output of erudition steeped in tradition and cooked with innovation. I was about to call this last aspect 'self-assertion', but it is more accurate to say that the componentry of Zimmerman's culture let him prime an embryonic self where his Dylan-persona was ready to emerge. And as that strange new self emerged so did the new songs, the new takes on his heritage.

By the time he was twenty, Dylan had heard more than a decade of nightly radio programs beaming into Hibbing, Minnesota. The radio schooled him in three centuries of the American Song, which in turn derived from further centuries of ancient madrigals and troubadour ditties—Scottish, Irish, German, African, Spanish, Jewish. With Dylan delving into this rag-and-bone shop of his Midwestern culture and his memory, a startling, fresh song like 'Highway 61' could get hot-rodded from street talk plus the Old Testament, music hall, carnival barkers' calls and English murder ballads.

This mode of composition is *rhapsodic*, in the original sense of the expression deriving from the two ancient Greek words *rhaptein* and *oide* denoting 'a sewn-together ode'. Extant elements get meshed and altered in the reiteration and recombination such that a startling new sonic fabric—stronger and more stimulant than the sum of its old parts—unfurls between the performer and the audience. This is the same kind of process that A. B. Lord examined in his classic *The Singer of Tales,* although Lord concentrated on the means whereby cultural memory stayed so strong that the variations of authorial originality were kept to an optimal minimum and song cycles were handed *intact* along generations for centuries.[3] Dylan operated on the other side of the schism that was made by modernism, where *innovation* was the animus. With modernism, originality trumped tradition because the objective was to make something astonishing and unprecedented.

Even so, the process started with tradition. As one of the definitive modernists, T. S. Eliot, explained in his canonical essay 'Tradition and the Individual Talent', the creative mind is best understood as a 'receptacle for storing up numberless feelings, phrases, images, which remain there until all the particles which can unite to form a new combination are present together'.[4] These particles can come from each individual's lived experience, but they are spawned as well in the culture that steeps every citizen's experience. And culture is nothing without the stored up remembrances that are structured by tradition. When creating original cultural work, Eliot contends, one dissolves into and rises up from tradition in such a way that the 'progress of an artist is…a continual extinction of personality' as one submits oneself to 'something which is more valuable'.[5]

This willing self-surrender is the obverse of the 'anxiety of influence' that Harold Bloom has controversially asserted to be the impetus of the great men who jostled for authority in the canon of twentieth-century English literature.[6] For thirty years or more, Bloom's theory drew disproportionate attention, but now in the age of digital culture Eliot's theory seems to have returned and grown more compelling as an account of creativity amidst all the mash-ups, the hiphop bites and the great, global bursts of poiesis that have generally become known as the aesthetics of remediation.[7] Borrowing from Eliot: the creator is best understood as a 'medium in which special, or very varied, feelings are at liberty to enter into new combinations'.[8] Whereas Bloom portrayed the great poets as *sui generis* entities struggling, Vulcan-like, to stoke atavistic fire for hammering paradigm-shifting creations out of their non-pareil subjectivities, Eliot's exemplary poets are not so much makers as melders who encourage their own disappearance, albeit momentarily, in order for distinctive new creations to get alloyed through themselves.

The new creation comes not from some *urwelt* where ever-originating inspiration burns, but from the everyday world where all that is extant is ready to be re-fashioned, including sentences, poems, artworks and myriad elements of culture that previous generations have produced and worked to preserve. From all that is extant, the culture makes the new things from the old things, *relationally*, as much as the artist does. Or to quote and endorse Robert Pogue Harrison's startling claim: '[all human cultures] compel the living to serve the interests of the unborn' such that 'culture perpetuates itself through the power of the dead'.[9]

So art comes from the transformation of given things, from relics and remembrances. And in that transformation there is usually a kind of *treason*, a *betrayal* of the given thing. By which I mean that in being tricked into a new form, the given thing becomes other to its original state. Treason, betrayal, traducement: these are usually thought to be sinister actions, coming from the wrong side of virtue, from leftfield, evincing insufficient reverence. But benefits can loom in such treasons. Consider the chance to remake a given thing by infusing it with new elements, by putting it in new relationships with other found and mutable things. Think of Dylan 'betraying' but also bowing down to Blind Willie McTell.

Etymologically, the French word for 'translation' (*'traduction'*) lurks close alongside the English word 'traduce'; and 'treason' (or *'trahison'* in French, which leads to the English word 'betrayal'). Treason's many variants echo through a translation because of the way the original thing can be betrayed, warped and abducted (as well as 'traducted') to a new state as it is moved from one language to another or from one medium or aesthetic form to another.

So I am proposing that wherever creativity roils, good can come from carefully traducing a given thing. Dylan's 'Like a Rolling Stone' can come from McTell's 'You Was Born to Die'. And the greatness of the original song stands firm even as the new song crashes into being.

The same goes for Christopher Logue's brazen 'War Music', which translates and betrays Homer's *Iliad* in the best possible way to make a vivid new evocation of warfare and state-sanctioned violence such that you can end up reading a gory-loud war-whoop encouraging you to imagine being a Trojan bovver-boy striding through 'noise so clamorous, it sucks'. With 'the Uzi shuddering against your hip' you can 'squeeze nickel through that rush of Greekoid scum'. And behold, you are remade even as the poem is transmogrified: 'Yourself another self you found at Troy'.[10]

This is more than a translation, of course. Although it starts out as that. Or more exactly, it starts out with Logue consulting reams of extant translations and then it gets wonderfully odder and more heretical. It is something other than Homer. It is a whole new thing, with Logue looking squarely at the catastrophe of modern times. And still, paradoxically, it comes from *The Iliad*. In translating it, Logue gets the original vividly 'wrong', but it is in precise accord with the original.

Think too of W. G. Sebald's investment in translation as a means to generate good strangeness and fresh insight. Sebald's control of the English language was supreme, yet he deliberately chose to write most of his works (even those aimed principally at an English-language readership) in German *and then to have them translated to English* through the creative agency of adroit writers (whom he appointed and painstakingly consulted) such as Michael Hulse and Anthea Bell. These relationships were not always smooth; indeed they were frequently acrimonious to the point of betrayal, with much traducing peppering the *traduction*, but from the trouble something valuable usually brewed. The translation-phase was one extra flush of creativity forced wilfully upon the drafts.

Thus far I have been extolling 'creative treason' by examining translations from language to language and from influential first-author to aspiring next-author. But what of the translation from medium to medium? Which is also to say from cognitive mode to cognitive mode, whereby the ideas and feelings that are couched in one medium and are appealing to one system of cerebral-and-affective appreciation are then translated to a different medium that galvanises other systems in one's intellection and sensorium.

One of my personal favourites in this multi-modal drift is Dave Hickey's dextrous essay 'A Life in the Arts', in which he analyses the influence of social and natural environments while orchestrating a sinuous, backcutting line of argument that investigates the languorous melodics in the trumpet-playing of Chet Baker. Intuiting that Baker's art is definitively Californian somehow, Hickey delves into the bodily pleasures of the sound, appreciating the way the listener is taken on a ride with the trumpeter's sparse glissandos and ethereal feints. Hickey notes how the flowing patterns of Baker's sound originate in the same lulling world that impels the 'cool economy and intellectual athletics of long-board surfing'![11]

When Californian board-riders translate the ocean swell, they utter a full incorporation with the sprit of their place; commensurately when Baker 'speaks' with his trumpet and his barely-breathed crooning, he utters the easeful sociability of bohemian communities strewn across LA and north along the Pacific Coast Highway, communities that take their tempo and mojo from the ocean. The surfers translate the fluid lineaments of the natural elements with their bodies, which are also their means of knowing and their medium of expression. Baker takes all this, adds a wary conviviality brought by his address to an audience, and he translates the full cool flux into sound via the artful movement of air.

Hickey notes how in each case—the surfing and the music—'a lost art of living in real time' is fashioned from the loll of experience. From one extant thing or system—ocean, breath, vibrational energy amongst elements and beings—constitutive factors are relationally realigned and translated so another thing arises. A fresh creation. Translating the surfers' arcs and scything cutbacks, Baker's trumpet glides out a keening gambit of oozed notes.

And *then,* in consideration and translation of these two mellifluous phenomena, Hickey makes his own original prose that is liquid and buoyant whilst also being dolorous and perspicacious. Consider, for example, this passage where he tells of the moments immediately after a friend has phoned him to say that Baker has died:

> I sat there for a long time in that cool, shadowy room, looking out at the California morning. I stared at the blazing white stucco wall of the bungalow across the street. I gazed at the coco palm rising above the bungalow's dark green roof. Three chrome-green, renegade parrots had taken up residence among its dusty fronds. They squawked and flickered in the sunshine.
>
> Above the bungalow, the parrots and the palm, the slate-gray pacific rose to the pale line of the horizon, and this vision of ordinary paradise seemed an appropriate, funereal vista for the ruined prince of West Coast cool.[12]

We know this writing is art because of the shift it makes in our understanding, and we know it is high quality. Let's waste no breath debating whether or not it is original or inspired. Hickey's prose in 'A Life in the Arts' comes from phenomena that already exist. It is informed and enriched by Hickey's attentiveness to local practices and environmental conditions that can be translated again and again—from anonymous surfers through Baker to Hickey—into new forms and insights. Hickey's prose resonates in that faculty of the reader which appreciates form as well as disquisition. And it lodges in a zone of consciousness other than the zones that Baker and the longboarders stimulate so slickly. What we have traced across these three expressive media is a run of translations through different cognitive modes, from the improvising board-riders to the tonal innovations of Baker, to the melodic analytics of Hickey. There is tradition here. Plus individual talent which finds and utters itself in the act of losing the original influence in the wash of the new relationships each author establishes amongst what already exists.

In some primers of aesthetics, this kind of translation would be called 'ekphrasis': the practice of glossing one mode of expression with another mode. Words rendering painting, for example, or music formed in response to dance. For me, the most galvanising version of this 'cognitive-mode translation' comes from the German philosopher, lawyer and filmmaker and avant-garde bureaucrat Alexander Kluge. (Note all his roles and the constant dodging, mode-shifting and translation that are required to help them make sense together. Vocational ekphrasis!)

Kluge has long espoused the power of silent cinema: not necessarily its market force; rather the imaginative élan in its subjective stimulus and intellectual fecundity. He maintains that the force of silent cinema comes from a definitive trope that operates as a run of cognitive shifts, which I summarise like this:

viewers encounter a pictorial sequence which is proffered for interpretation as the sequence gathers its duration and complexity; after due consideration, the viewers generate their interpretations of the meaning and system of feelings within the sequence; then an inter-title presents words (appealing to a cognitive mode that is radically different from the pictorial and proprioceptive faculties that the movie sequence has been agitating thus far); this linguistic sense contends with the interpretation that the viewers have just supplied for themselves; *and then* the viewers are obliged to decide whether to accept the proffered interpretation or to adapt or stay true to the one they invented on their own.

And then another sequence runs past.

Thus throughout a silent movie viewers are goaded to know their own minds, to use their minds to make versions of sense and to know that every mind in the cinema has several profusely generative modes whirring in it at any one time, even as the filmmaker also contends with the meanings by providing the inter-titles as guidelines for interpretation.

With silent cinema an audience is therefore an imaginative, disputatious and discursive assembly. The audience is a sceptical and *politicised* assembly, therefore. And the contentious significance of the film—simultaneously intellectual and emotional—comes from each viewer's speculative psychology contending in sceptical sociability with every other self in the cinema (including the filmmaker's self, of course) as images and words roll around each other, offering different, medium-specific grasps on experience.[13] On the screen and inside each viewer's sensibility, moving images and words translate the represented experience back and forth

Self Extraction

across each other. In order to know what is being represented, each viewer has to extract an authoring self from this tumult.

The authoring self: we have come back to this figure by examining what occurs when you become a highly participant viewer or reader translating across media and drawing lines of new understanding out of memory and tradition. The authoring self. It might be useful now if I report on my own experience as an ekphrastic author, offering a brief account of the process of translating pictorial qualities into language and back again. I hope it is a modest, close-witness account of how a portion of individual talent can extract itself and then assert itself in response to the given world, the world of tradition, of extant things.

My account focuses on *Accident Music*, another iteration from the *Life After Wartime* suite of works that have been examined in previous chapters. In this suite, aesthetic factors such as sounds, images, rhythm and routines of re-framing within a forensic photography archive are brought together to manifest in the perceiver a sense of how meanings and emotional charge can burst out from the images all these year later. Detailing life in Sydney during the decades immediately after World War II, the pictures portray the city in a pained and piquant way that contradicts but also complements the promise of pleasure that is the clichéd understanding of the city. Mulling over the photographs, you comprehend the liveliness of the place better because the pictures thrum not only with heat and light and the vitality of the street but also with mendacity and mortality. The pictures help you see some of the social and historical forces that swell sombre beneath the shimmers.

And the pictures call for language. Repeatedly I find myself responding to some pictorial quality or some shift of hue by translating it into a phrase that needs to be more evocative and sensuous than descriptive. So in *Accident Music*, I use each photo as a stimulus for poetry which is drawn from the receptacle of images, experiences, readings, viewings and writing that make up my self. I use the words to simmer the picture in some new way so the perceiver can extract some extra qualities from the imagery and, by extension, from the actual, habitable scenes being represented. The language is meant to gloss photography directly; but it is also meant to re-illuminate the city, and to extract surprising qualities and conjunctions of memory and insight from my ever-altering self.

An example is this picture from a 1954 'Manslaughter' file (FP09_080_008).

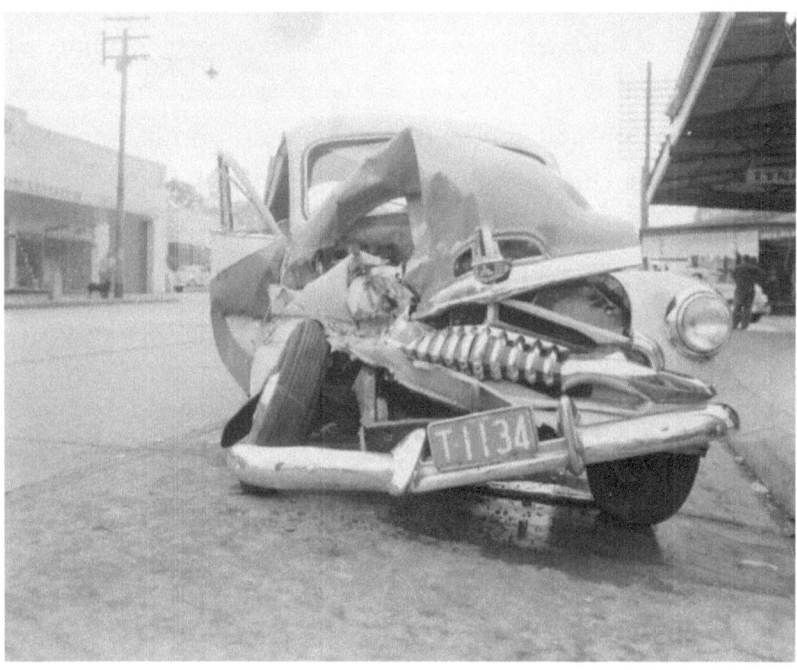

Some of the striking qualities in the image are: the hot light and the cool shade; the folded softness of the wreck that warps around the pliant rubber tyre and makes a paradox with the bleak metal in the panels and bumper bars; the slump; the escaping ooze of oil and gasoline, haptic and olfactory; the headache waiting to burgeon; the silence lurking as a daze after recent horrible clamour; the stillness following kinetic havoc. And much else besides, including a terribly tender sense of mortality and surrender.

So, I offer sets of utterances—phrases that sit alongside the image, matching the picture's size in a diptych and making an ekphrastic partnership for your linguistic and imagistic systems of cognition. Sets of three utterances like these:

See how an object can take the shape of a scream.
Understand that vim can ebb in a warm sluice.
Accept that heat is just a brief sigh made by cold.

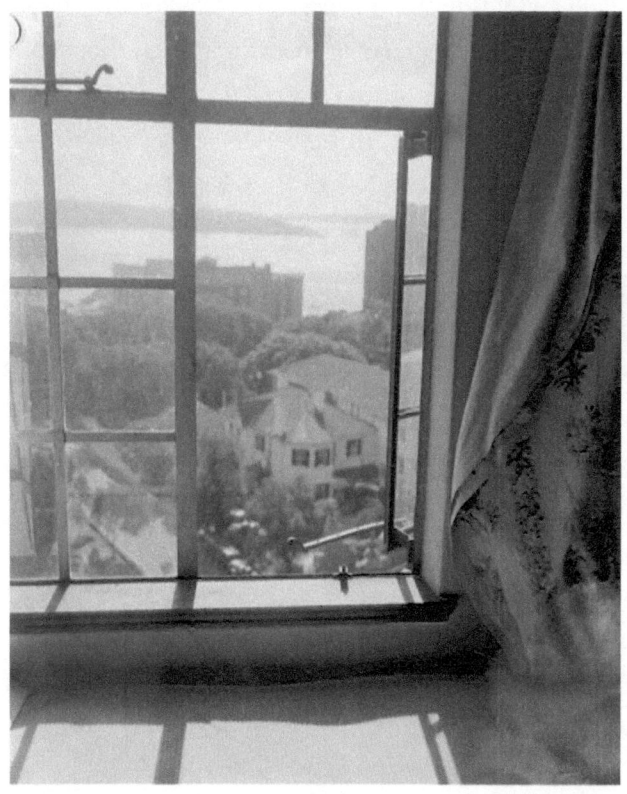

Another example is this interior scene (FP08_068_002—'Suspicious Death'), where longing and some promise of release contend with a terrible void that makes a picture that is equally light and ponderous: a picture of gravity. In front of this image, I get almost every sense of that word and that feeling: *gravity*.

How to give language to this image, when it offers so much? Here are three breaths of my written speech, translating the picture, and perhaps betraying my self:

Each night the town holds a new lover in thrall.
Lean out past the old thresholds.
Feel how the breeze wants you and offers an embrace.

I have made a few hundred of these diptychs, in the *Accident Music* series.[14] They give me a chance to extract an author from myself by setting my individual, stored experiences in resonance with the traditions and the sensory impacts—of crime, of crime writing, of documentary photography, of city-wandering, of elegy and epitaph—that have been made both in me and in a larger world cohering through time.

So by way of conclusion, I hope this much is clear now: resonance and amplification can be made with the act of translation, by betraying some extant thing whilst simultaneously glossing and revering it too. A new thing gets to emerge in and through the author's self while whatever talent lurks in the author's individuality contends with the cunning of the world and all its media and sensory modes.

Think of Bob Dylan translating Blind Willie McTell. Think of Christopher Logue betraying Homer in the most honourable manner. Think of yourself finessing anything that moves you and that makes itself available, through tradition, for the good reason it needs or lures out from you.

Notes

1 See http://www.theparisreview.org/interviews.
2 B. Dylan, *Chronicles: volume one*, Simon & Schuster, New York, 2005, p. 228.
3 A. B. Lord, *The Singer of Tales*, Oxford University Press, London, 1961.
4 T. S. Eliot, 'Tradition and the Individual Talent' in *The Sacred Wood: essays on poetry and criticism*, Alfred A. Knopf, New York, 1921, p. 49.
5 Eliot, 'Tradition and the Individual Talent', p. 47.
6 H. Bloom, *The Anxiety of Influence: a theory of poetry*, Oxford University Press, London, 1973.
7 J. Bolter and R. Grusin, *Remediation: understanding new media*, MIT Press, Cambridge, MA, 1999.
8 Eliot, p. 48.
9 R. P. Harrison in *The Dominion of the Dead*, The University of Chicago Press, Chicago, 2003, p. ix.
10 C. Logue, *All Day Permanent Red: The First Battle Scenes of Homer's Iliad Rewritten, Part One*, Faber and Faber, London, 2003, p. 29.
11 D. Hickey, 'A Life in the Arts' in *Air Guitar: essays on art & democracy*, Art Issues Press, Los Angeles, 1997, p. 77.
12 Hickey, 'A Life in the Arts', p. 73.
13 A. Kluge, W. Reinke, E. Reitz and M. Hansen (trans.), 'Word and Film' in *October, vol. 46, Alexander Kluge: Theoretical Writings, Stories, and an Interview* (autumn, 1988), MIT Press, Boston, pp. 83–95.
14 See an account of them here: http://www.rossgibson.com.au.

10

WHERE THE DARKNESS LOITERS

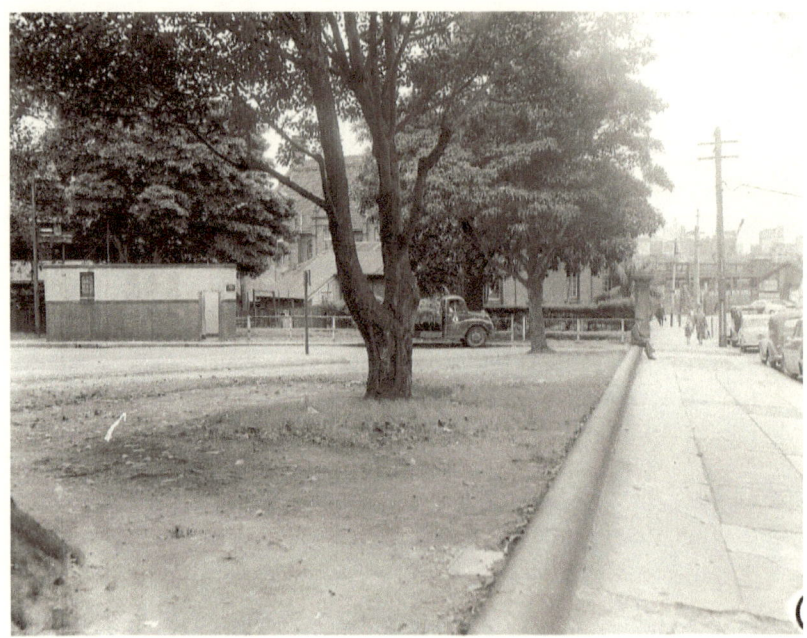

Notice the superbly controlled tensions in this image? The composition torqued around the central tree; the welted concrete border that holds the park and the street so closely opposed; the dusty heat of the concrete city fizzing into the cooler 'green' on the other side of the dividing line; the man perched athwart that line; the machine motoring through the green on its way back to the grey; the harsh toilet block—a massed and pungent chunk of city—clamping the barely organic ground as if governing the paltry nature of the place. Notice, also, the question posed by the aesthetics of the foreground: where do I, the viewer, stand in relation to this 'nature', this 'culture' and this scar of division that scythes toward me as I contemplate the scene?

For as long as I look at it or remember it, this image unsettles me in the way its composition is so brittle, ready as it is to craze at several points of stress. With all its formal emphasis on composure and regulation, the image also 'tells' of doubt, denial and forgetting.

It is a police forensic photograph from Sydney in the 1950s. An intelligent image, disconcerting and sophisticated. In the attic of Sydney's Justice and Police Museum there are thousands like it. Myriad images covering transgression and detection in the harbour city.

The men who made these pictures conducted a cumulative, intuitive survey of a society enduring flushes of desire and fear in the aftermath of World War II. Every day, the photographers drove motorbike sidecars to scenes of outbursts, accidents and mysteries. They documented bruised places where the arbitrary settings of law had momentarily slipped and unmanageable forces of living had sloshed about. Usually the photographers were among the first people to enter the scene after some transgression had electrified it, and often they found themselves in locations of great 'spiritual' force—sites that were both disturbed and disturbing—where incursions from the other side of supposed decency had taken place. Occasionally they produced uncanny images that reached out of the prosaic to grasp and display something else.

The police photographers were practical men, unsentimental servants of regulation and plain-speaking, yet they repeatedly transcended their workaday tasks even as they fulfilled them. In the haphazard archive that they left behind, there are many images that can only be described as aesthetic, exquisite as they are grim. I particularly remember one file about a man who suicided in the public toilet of a Redfern park—he had wrapped his head in a hessian bag of gelignite and sparked it with a car battery. Out of the violence of this act, the photographer produced something more than just a record of remains. Legally unpublishable at present, the appalling images relating to this case are prosaic court documents, but they can also be interpreted as an essay about a determination to know sadness, ugliness and horror without blinking and without exploiting the dignity of the 'object' that has to be known.

Walking daily into such spiritually fraught situations, many of the photographers were able to summon an aesthetic facility which they deployed to extend their job past measuring and collecting. Occasionally they responded to a crime scene with so much nuance that the space they portrayed appears ethical as well as physical; and sometimes there seems to be a glimmer of the metaphysical in there too. Almost all of the photographers were able, occasionally, to witness and communicate complex, ambiguous and unspeakable insights.

When I open the files sixty years later, the images still simmer to remember the experiences these men and their cameras absorbed. Call the men cops, call them scientists (their institutional acronym was SIB: Scientific Investigation Branch), call them artists—in all their roles they sensed covert patterns in their suffering city, and they found ways to deepen the soundings of their evidentiary searches, to witness some weightless mood or spirit of the times. The resulting pictures were often divinations, therefore, registering repulsions, compulsions and illegitimacies that surged through their environments and through their fellow citizens (and through themselves also, most likely.) Today, the photographs offer us an unreasonable history of Sydney—a report from the edges of approved and regular behaviour, a report from the places where tidy moral and philosophical categories are blurring.

When a great river reaches the sea, it continues to behave like a river, maintaining its current and momentum through the engulfing water that will eventually subsume it.[1] It agitates and influences long after it appears to have finished. This is the nature of historic experiences also. Consider a war in a city, for example. Once the tumult has eased into the apparent stillness of peace, old surges of trauma and impulse can persist implicitly, long after the explicit upheavals have disappeared.

In Sydney, for ten or fifteen years after the end of World War II, the city pulsed with many 'underworld' forces and enigmas that were continuations of pathologies and libidinous freedoms that had flourished unpoliced during the war years, when authorities had been concentrating on the victory campaign. During the 1950s, the 'unregulated' morality that developed during wartime did not disappear. The clichéd, wholesome life often ascribed to the 1950s is barely visible in the police pictures. A full decade after D-Day, the sexual adventures and the taste for alternative forms of domesticity and salary that had burgeoned during the blackouts were still active throughout the city. Transgressions continued apace. There was so much to get away with under cover of the normalcy that is supposed to have snuggled back down once peace and right behaviour were ruling again. After all, this was a decade of distressing uncertainty as well as promise, a time full of blind spots when Sydney mutated quickly and forcefully, shedding its economic reliance on the British economy and embracing US dollars and popular culture, at the same time as the geography of the city was altered by the beginnings of the car culture and profiteered suburban haemorrhaging that have paralysed it today. This was also a time when the police department expanded rapidly and systems of corruption involving politicians and criminal organisations began to taint the force as deeply as ever; perhaps even more than during the convicts' days, when the system of corruption binding policing to liquor, gambling, land-seizure and political opportunism had been made normal and continuous in the town. For all the simple nostalgia that gets foisted on the 1950s, this was no innocent time. The good old days did not happen here, while wholesome family values and government probity were always limned with something darker.

The SIB photos show the ethical and emotional restlessness that troubled the everyday lives of many Sydney-siders in those days. The files abound with poisonings and *crimes de passion*, frauds, bigamy, railway sabotage, sedition, illicit abortions, suicides, carnal knowledge and sundry 'perversions', so-called in the files. Admittedly, any sizeable record of crime is going to emphasise aberration, violence and socio-pathology, but the criminal history of Sydney during the 1950s presents a city strikingly scored by fractious acts of desire, moral ambiguity and the inability to forget whatever gets denied or ignored. With the enigmas recorded by the photographers—in court these enigmas get called 'clues'—memories get siphoned out of hunches, glimpses and intuitions. Dumb evidence mutters before becoming eloquent. A memory is a translation—from a cryptic scratch or an object lying misplaced over to an hypothesis and an argument—from chunks and particles of matter sprawled in portentous physical relationships all parlayed into discourse carrying a backstory from denial or attempted erasure through to judgement in the public forum. *Forensic* judgement in, for and by the forum.

The pictures also show that there was within the police force a compulsion to seek out 'deviants' and definition-testers. With hindsight it looks as if the lawmakers often produced the lawbreakers. The investigators produced the concealers. Whichever ways the cases arose, though, the crime-scene photos tell of a city somewhat agog with transgression, aberration, blinking in and out of amnesia.

Sensing the undercurrents of the times, many forensic photographers put the quandaries into their pictures. Or more precisely, they found ways to highlight quandaries that were already there—albeit occulted—in the scenes they encountered. I am thinking not only of the secular mysteries of whodunit crimes, but also of moral and philosophical perplexity. Some photographers looked past the empirical evidence they were required to deliver. For example, hundreds of pictures in the Justice and Police archive are shaped by an almost obsessive attention to borderlines: thresholds between houses and gardens, the verge made by a riverbank, the indistinct smear of a harbour foreshore, shadowy vestibules in apartment buildings, tunnel entrances, the void on the far-side of a cliff, the lee-side of a retaining wall, half-wooded knolls in parks and reserves. The divisions are often symbolic as well as literal: by fixing on scenes of transitional activities, many photographers evoked the porous distinctions between 'right' and 'wrong' behaviour, between the approved world and the underworld, between life and death, between desire and perversion, between sexual categories, between innocence and suspicion. And yes, in many of the images, this blurring is shown explicitly at some cusp between 'nature' and 'culture'. In part, this cusp is where the acts themselves have occurred, but in part also the cusp is emphasised with a kind of poetic licence that indicates that the photographer wants to bear witness to the ambiguities and indeterminacies that pulse like nature through the city.

For example, there are hundreds of abortion files in the archive and the scenes—ordinary rooms of ordinary people—are photographed in such a way that they show banality in concert with an underlying spiritual tension. Living Rooms + Life Contending with Death + Police = Domestic Mysticism.

However, the most arresting renditions of a city fuzzed with indistinction are found not in the abortion pictures, but in a set of files that I've come to know as the 'park pictures'. These are images collected as evidence relating to a range of activities named as sex crimes, mostly homosexual dalliance or 'trade'. Now, there is no dispute that some parks and the public lavatories therein were (and remain) 'beat' locations. Parks truly are places poised between nature and culture, between the wild and the managed, just as they also exist between shadow and glare, the private and the public, silence and assignation. Therefore parks simply are good dramatic settings for brief flarings of anonymous and ambiguously defined sex. Even so, in these pictures from the 1950s, the parks of Sydney become metaphors as well as locations. The way they get framed and toned, the parks (and especially the environs around the pavilions and lavatories therein) become correlatives of compulsions and phobias that were tempering the decade. In particular, the images catch an edginess about the way civil behaviour always seems to be assailed by unruly urges and 'indecorous' appetites, the way 'waste' and 'recreation' confuse and impel each other. In other words, many of the pictures are shaped by the worry that culture will not hold and that our nature—human as it is—will spill out illicitly and betray itself as unclean, uncontrolled or unquenchable.

A sense of dread usually gets composed in the aesthetics of the park pictures—sometimes in the contrast of heavy shade pushing against light; often in the ominously deserted compositions so recently jostled by people jog-trotting away from a trauma or a delicious moment of shame. And in the pictures that are not threatened with darkness, there tends to be a cauterising glare that overwhelms the scene as if we have arrived immediately after some heat-flash of unreason. Almost invariably, the overall impression is that this 'aftermath' scene has been shocked out of composure by a culture whose nature is more ugly and savage and abiding than peaceable citizens are prepared to admit.

Denial and forgetting are disallowed by the pictures. To use the language of 1950s psychiatry, the park photographs are panicked by some visualised energy of the id, a ravenous force that seems to course like a greedy inheritance through the city and its people, a force that erupts all the more vehemently because it has to repulse the 'right behaviour' that pretends to contain it. In this sense the park scenes can be interpreted as Cold War images—fearful, maniacally vigilant yet also perversely enthralled by the attractions of darkness, of an oblivion that is loitering nearby whenever the camera grabs at the light buffeting the dark in a scene.

The power of these images is partly that they call out several personae who fleetingly inhabit both yourself and the scenes in front of you: musing on the pictures, you can imagine the photographer, the perpetrator, the victim, the bystander—and perhaps you can also sense the place itself as an entity with a history, a remembering spirit or consciousness.

When you encounter the park pictures, you find yourself warped into many new dispositions and temporary identities, some of them fearful, all of them formed by the way the photographer has chosen to render the scene. In these places, as they are represented in the photographs, you can detect old abominations and continuous compulsions that extend past yourself at the same time as you know yourself to be at the very centre of the disturbing force that gets generated in the interplay between image and viewer. Within yourself you feel the trouble and outrage that once seared the scene. In this way the pictures are haunting; they possess you and pass through you like some ineffable and elemental alarm-signal.

The parks are actual places where some citizens go to relax their more constrained selves and where others loosen their urges and insufficiencies. The photographs show memory and desire are mixed in the emulsion. The scenes are real places. But they are more than that. They are also symbolic settings where the police photographers saw and displayed some of the tensions organising their times. The park pictures show places simultaneously without firm definition and with too many definitions. Consider the groves, the pathways, the untended pagodas, ponds and swimming pools. Adorned by all these liminal features that lead to somewhere less regulated, the parks allow people to ease into immersions, to enjoy temporary change or suspension before emerging and rejoining regularity. Depicting these features, the park pictures wrench us back and forth across the verge that we inhabitants of culture like to use as a fence around a more elemental kind of force, a force that manifests itself in bodily agitation and emotion, in fluids, in the surprising surge of an unbidden memory, in light shifts, in burgeon and decay—all the motilities that welcome and unsettle us in the places we visit to let rectitude slip.

Looking again at the files that I have set aside, I am simultaneously compelled and appalled by the verges, vestibules and transitionary spots and moments that loiter between the categories of nature and culture that are visible here. This is why, finally, I cannot tidy up my responses to the park pictures. They offer me ambivalence, flashes of recall and speculation, subjective instability and a failure of poise and proper behaviour. Therein lies their power—they show me what I want and what I want not to see.

Notes
1   Thanks to Noel Sanders, in conversation, for this insight.

11

PALPABLE HISTORY

Imagine some undocumented circumstance. A situation that deserves or needs witnessing. Imagine it is an aftermath with no adequate residue of the *textual* kinds of records that are conventionally used for tracing what happened, for making traditional history of it. Say these records have gone missing or were never gathered. Now imagine that some *non-textual* traces of this circumstance have persisted from the past. For example, some such traces prevail not in documents but in photographs. Or, just as likely, you might detect the traces in landscapes, or as gouges and smears on buildings, as intensities or contusions in human bodies, as rituals or figures of speech in family tales and personal memories.

Given such circumstances, is there something we can do to grasp the forces that have pushed out of the past and are shaping the world now? If you are deprived of written accounts, or if you are disinclined to offer writing as your historical practice, what aspects of the past can still be evoked with valid historicist intent? Say, in audio-visual formats, by utilising photographs and videos in temporal sequences and spatial installations? What role might such non-verbal events and proclamations play in offering some persuasive, deeply felt insights into the way the past seems to flow through the present toward the future?

These questions call for a mode of historiography that appeals to the senses. We need non-textual (but designed and structured) patterns of propositions about the past, propositions that register in the nervous system, that register as pulses, flows, rhythms and lapses, that are registered first as mood and emotion and then lead to intellection. Propositions not for the page but for audio-visual devices or for exhibition spaces and performance schedules. Perceiving such propositions, you might get convinced 'in your bones' before drawing on the portions of our sensibility that manage linguistic, textual argument.

This attentiveness to *felt conviction* leads to a couple more questions, which challenge the precepts of conventional historiography. First, where in your consciousness, in your sensorium, can conviction lodge? Second, what might it mean if a convincing proposition takes the form of a structured feeling rather than an argument? Or to ask this another way, can you 'tell' a history that has conviction but no particular, semantic *meaning*? Can you tell history which gives you a feeling rather than a message?

All these questions challenge discourse with rhetoric; they all disturb reason with affect. They are questions concerned with feeling, with sensing what urge or animus moves through a scene and through time. They are questions concerned with how vital an event or topic might be. So, they are concerned firstly with detecting *how* vital a force might be and secondly with detecting how one gets a sense *in* the vitals.

But enough with the abstractions. I should offer a specific example: the particular instance that started me thinking about these modes of non-verbal, 'meaningless' but palpable historiography.

In 2004, with cinematographer Ben Speth, I made an artwork called *Street X-Rays*.[1] It is a spatial installation comprised of surround sound and five video screens suspended in a pattern such that the viewer can never see all five screens at any one time.

Investigating the room, the viewer is encouraged by the layout to adopt ever-new vantage points, to assemble different configurations of relationships, screen-to-screen, whilst all the time understanding that there is no singularly privileged, all-seeing point where the entire installation might be available to one sovereign scope. Meanwhile the sound swirls around and through you. A restless, investigative viewer, you quickly understand that the scene can only be known partly and in passing – in motion, through motion and as motion.

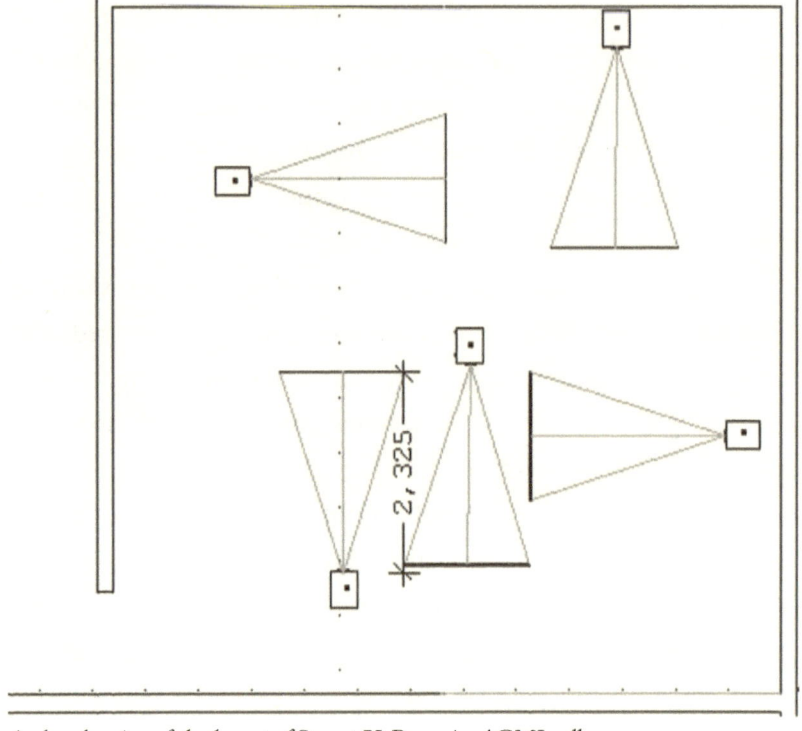

A plan drawing of the layout of Street X-Rays *in ACMI gallery.*

On each of the five screens is a diptych. One side of the diptych shows a black-and-white crime-scene photograph from

Sydney in the 1950s; the other side shows colour video footage with live-location sound depicting the same scene fifty years later. You get twenty seconds of such a pairing, with the screen showing the passage of fifty years, from the black-and-white historical photograph over to its contemporary kinetic counterpart. Then that pairing fades to black and a new pairing replaces it as, on the luminous screen, a different pulse of historical time takes place. Likewise, all the other screens are receiving similar ebbs and flows of time and place, thus making the installation an active, changeful thing with several places and times alive in it at all times.

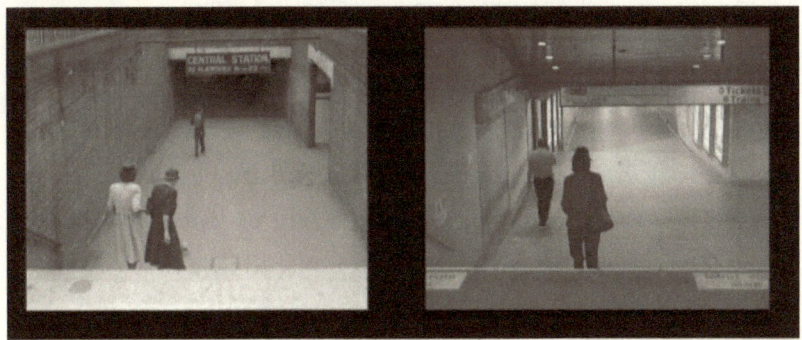

A diptych from Street X-Rays.

Viewed all together as an aesthetic system, the five screens assemble a shifting audio-visual version of a city composed by spatial, temporal, graphical, kinetic and thematic relationships. See the cars, the architecture, the advertising. See the way people stand, how they walk, their relationships to vehicles, to doorways, to one another. See how these relationships change over time, how closely men stood in groups during the 1950s, how chary men are of each other now in public spaces.

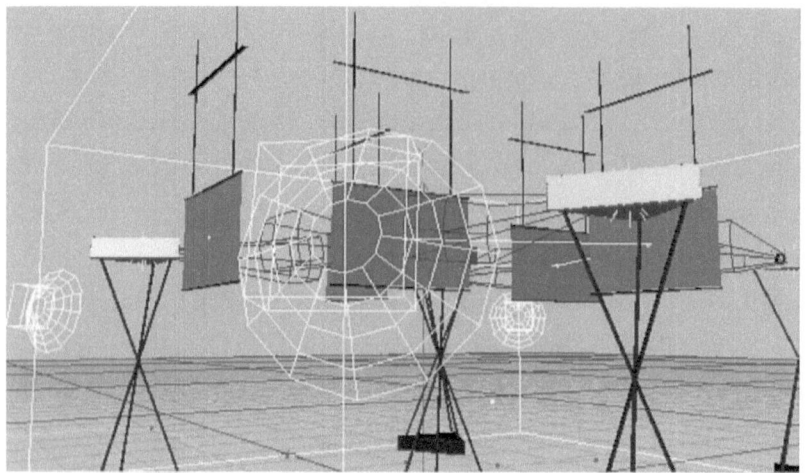

A wireframe rendition of the viewer's perspective in Street X-Rays.

From any one vantage point in the installation, the viewer is able to see, at most, eight framed images, all of which are tending to form relationships in space and time. Well, they are tending to form, but they are also tending to lose form, as each on-screen sequence drops away and is replaced by a new one (even though the old one gets held in your memory for a time), while the entire installation stipples with little sequenced instabilities of appearance-and-disappearance. And all around, the massed sound of the several video sequences plus a minimal mood-music soundtrack continue to envelop the viewer with a 'meta-level' fullness-of-scene that seems to be heard entirely but can never be seen fully.

At its first exhibition, *Street X-Rays* worked well enough, pretty much as I had hoped and expected. Except I became aware of a couple of features (as always happens when artistic practice is treated as research) that were unexpected and gratefully accepted. These little revelations started me thinking more seriously about historical *feeling* rather than *meaning*, about historical affect rather than argument.

Palpable History

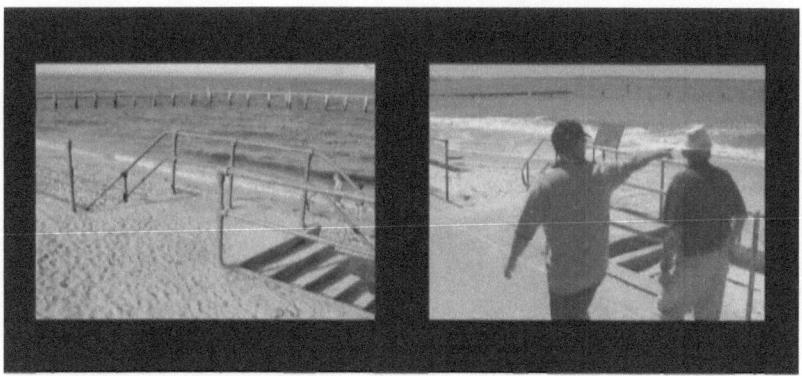

A diptych from Street X-Rays.

First, because the screens are made with a translucent material allowing simultaneous front and back projection, a percentage of the beams from the projectors penetrate through the screens and cast careening ghost-scenes on the surrounding walls of the gallery. These ghost-scenes imply an immense and extensive world unbounded by the gallery, and they swirl at odd angles so that the entire gallery feels slightly vertiginous from time to time, as if the room is swallowing the viewer while the world itself is swallowing the room. You feel buffets of historical turbulence unsettle the room. You feel caught in the installation's surges, at the behest of the scenes' combinative energies and time folds and flows so that you feel something like a force of history buffeting your whole world. It is real, this feeling; you get it inside yourself. The artwork produces it for you. It is a feeling that makes a quandary leading to an implicit kind of knowledge. It is not an argument, this feeling. It is not even a proposition. It is palpable and it helps you think about the presence of the past in ordinary time, and in you, and in the larger world that holds you and reacts to you. It gets you thinking about how dynamically interfused everything is: yourself, the larger world and all its tempos and urges. Perhaps it's better to call this an *awareness*, implicit as it is, rather than *knowledge*, which implies a proposition made explicit and verbally communicable.

The second surprising effect in *Street X-Rays* is a kind of 'vectoral continuity' that asserts itself at unpredictable moments in the darkened space-and-time that floats *between* the screens, in the gallery's 'negative space'. The effect works like this: in the video footage on one screen, a car will drive past or someone will walk or run or ride a bike across and out of the frame. This traveller's trajectory – this *vector* with its accompanying soundtrack – throws your attention into the black-and-white photograph alongside, where the traveller is now submerged elsewhere in time but is implied nevertheless to your imagination despite being invisible. Then the moving figure turns up – transmogrified from man-in-car to woman-on-bike, let's say – on another screen, in another location. The town writhes with historicised actions. To borrow some oddly compelling verbiage from James Agee to evoke this wonderment, the immersed viewer gets to sense how every present moment is 'from all sides streamed inward upon, bombarded, pierced, destroyed by that enormous sleeting of all objects forms and ghosts how great how small no matter', which makes the world a restless event suffused by all that has gone before.[2]

Watching and hearing this happen, you feel the paradox of the simultaneous presence-and-absence of the figure that has been so animated in one moment and so evanescent in the next. You feel different time layers and historical factors fold dynamically into each other and you sense that you have gained an intuitive grasp of an irrational notion: that all times and characters from the past are equally available to each other and to you, all at once, if only you can develop the faculties for being aware of them. You trust this kinetically derived feeling, this trace that you *feel* before you know it, this trace of the vector's presence now past. You acknowledge that the vector has *optically* disappeared once it has exited the video frame, but you sense its continuation despite its disappearance. You feel it play through your embodied imagination, not only via the parts of you that have electrical flashes or endocrinal flushes moving along them but also via the awareness you have of how you yourself can move through the places of the world through time.

The vector is there and not there, troubling your present reason with your persisting sensation of these events that have just been occurring and are continuing to occur, albeit invisibly and 'undocumented'. The event might be gone momentarily but it remains too, moving through your activated and time-aware sensorium. The installation gives you this sense of historical continuity. It attunes you to this flux – this 'urge' in history that is so immaterial yet so palpable – that is partly witnessed and partly imagined in space across time.

Meanwhile, the surrounding sound tells you of other actions all occurring, unviewed but undeniable, outside of your immediate optical scope. And as you notice all this happen, again and again, across the configuration of screens, you begin to feel convinced that this shifting, partial city is threaded through with constantly appearing-and-disappearing forces which are moving and connecting from scene to scene and time to time, forces which are only occasionally visible but are constantly operational and fleetingly perceptible. You sense the absences too: the fact of them, not only how present these absences are but also how they are hatched across with tendencies and trajectories, with the kind of historical momentum that saturates large, historically governed environments such as the city that is being represented and investigated in the artwork.

Thus you feel a forceful world of historical tendency moving around you. Indeed, because you follow the vector and imagine its continuity whenever you cannot see it, you realise that you are moving with it and therefore this historical force is moving *as* you as well as *through* you. You are part of this systematically enlivened world of vectors appearing, disappearing but ever-present. You receive the vectors *and* you are a vector too.

Then you begin to feel that you have become more than just a viewer. You have taken the role of a *sensor*, relying on convictions and sensations that are registering for you in unaccustomed faculties. As a sensor, you trust that there is a perceptible world available to your as-yet unaccustomed senses. You begin to entertain notions; for example that you might learn to imagine and understand certain propositions *haptically* and *via proprioception* rather than just *visually* or *semantically*, and that you might get a *choreographic divination* rather than a *surveillant reading* of the town, that you might never know the town's meanings but you might divine some of its tendencies. And that this too is historical awareness. And on reflection, over time, it might even become knowledge.

Aided by the flux dramatised in such audio-visual systems, you might transcend what you cannot *see* or *read* in and about the kinetic-spatial system of the city. You might feel and thereby imagine the dynamics of the place. You might become convinced in your senses, convinced about the existence of certain structuring forces that are prevalent and dynamic in the city that is represented in *Street X-Rays*. This conviction is not reasonable, admittedly. Rather, it is a sluice of urgency felt in the glands, a pulse of electricity zinging the nerves. But it is historical awareness made palpable, and it feels convincing, this encounter with dynamic historical tendencies, no matter how invisible or illegible they might be.

All this feels *unreasonably* convincing, for it is not playing out according to the clean ratios of logical intellect. You feel you have made contact with something emphatic and emotionally comprehensible about the city, about how it is a reservoir and a transponder for time, space and human energies surging across districts and decades. You feel convinced by this proposition, that the past is always abroad in our present-day experience. For example, if *Street X-Rays* helps you sense that a vector or historical tendency can appear and disappear but is always implied in the 'thickened' time-space of the city's everyday life, well surely other forces such as systems of political power, habits, emotions, fears and aspirations could all be felt flowing through past and present configurations of our habitable world. And surely this is no pointless exercise, to find the cultural means to help people become aware of this sense of historical continuity, to know it in their bones, in their glands and nerves? Such an artwork makes no lucid arguments, but it does create an awareness where ignorance or insouciance are usually encouraged. Awareness and argument – different but related.

Historians have traditionally maintained suspicion over aesthetics and rhetoric. Because aesthetics appeals, by dictionary definition, to everything that is 'perceptible by the senses', and because rhetoric is a technique of persuasion tapping feelings rather than cerebration, the affective register of aesthetics is generally considered too louche, too unaccountable for valid historical discourse.[3] But if discourse is meant to lead to conviction, must this conviction be evacuated of affection? For example, if no one *cares* about a conviction, if no one feels its urgent rightness in their desirous person, well, is that conviction likely to lead to any valuable action in the larger world? Is it likely to have any historic outcome? Who will care enough to bear witness to the prevalence of the past? Without personal affect, what social effect?

Please note that I am not arguing that conventional, text-based history is useless. I am saying it is only partially useful. Just as imaginative speculation and aesthetic appreciation are only partially useful. Altogether, though, they might be productive, if we found rigorous ways to loosen and interlace the borders between 'proper' historiography and affective speculation and appreciation.

When responding to the sense of the urgency that one can feel when witnessing the present traces of our past, I always think of the great, unconventional historian Greg Dening, when he used to proclaim that the most important historical work happens when scholars apply imagination to evidence. *Imagination*, not *fantasy*, he used to stress, always asserting that one needs to retain an allegiance but not a craven fealty to the evidence.[4] (I examine the work of Dening in more detail in a later chapter.) A fiction-teller is not obliged to do this; the fiction-teller makes a different contract with the audience. But no matter what medium is being utilised in the artwork, the historically informed artist maintains an allegiance to traces that have been touched by the world. If this does not make the artist an historian – strictly defined – it does make for a historical understanding that the artist can generate. A palpable history, in other words. A palpable history, often without words.

So to conclude but also to acknowledge, understand and perhaps even to appreciate the inconclusiveness, here is the trickiest and most important point of this essay: the conditions of living and working in an aftermath-culture like Australia are such that a great deal of the vital evidence is either missing or non-textual and the evidence that we do have is often partial, broken or obscured by denials. Which means that conventional historiographical protocols often come up short when we try to get the fullest possible comprehension of the past that has whelped our present.

In aftermath cultures like Australia we need to imagine across gaps and quandaries in the evidence; we need to venture out past the vestiges or documented ruses that have been allowed some visibility, past what is accepted as admissible for discursive conviction. In thinking venturesomely like this, the first task for the sceptical imagination is to find ways to heighten our awareness of the prevalence of implicit historical forces. For without this awareness, so many different kinds of historiography are unthinkable. And plainly, there is yet so much more to imagine about the persistence of the past in our present. As the Stoics proclaimed all those centuries ago (stoically understanding that the majority of citizens usually wish not to know this), 'everything exists in the present, even the past'.[5] Why not try to imagine all the ways it might be possible to grasp how that ancient truth feels nowadays?

Notes

1. M. Stubbs (ed. and curator), *Proof: the act of seeing with one's own eyes*. Australian Centre for the Moving Image, Melbourne, December 2004 – March 2005. See http://www.acmi.net.au/proofexhibition.jsp. Also, see catalogue: Mike Stubbs (ed.), *Proof: the act of seeing with one's own eyes*, 96 pp colour paperback, ISBN 1 920805 07 9.
2. J. Agee and W. Evans, *Let us Now Praise Famous Men*, Houghton Mifflin, Boston, 1988, (first published 1941), p. 110.
3. G. A. Wilkes and W. A. Krebs (eds) *Collins English Dictionary*, 3rd edition, Harper Collins, Sydney, 1991, p. 24.
4. See G. Dening, http://www.nla.gov.au/events/history/papers/Greg_Dening.html, accessed 29 April 2007.
5. B. Cache, *Earth Moves: the furnishing of territories*, MIT Press, 1995, p. 22.

12

POLITICS, POETICS AND POLICING

In 1944, with the Allied war effort finally gathering hope, Robert Menzies contributed the first chapter in a book of polemical essays that were organised under the title *Post-war Reconstruction in Australia*. Fidgeting in Parliamentary Opposition at the time, Menzies needed to keep himself big in electors' minds. Nowadays nobody expects an aspiring prime minister to associate with views as challenging and contentious as the ones that tangled in the pages following Menzies' introduction. But the world was so pained and perplexed then, and the future was so wide open and urgent, most people agreed the full gamut of outlooks demanded serious consideration. Exuberant simplicity would not win the day and Menzies needed a platform for displaying the reach of his intellect. So, despite his conservative preferences, he was keen to engage with the grand visions and radical stocktakes that jostled in the book.

This explains Menzies' readiness to consort in the book with a chapter as wilful as 'The Change-over to Peace' by D. B. Copland, who was the economics advisor to prime minister John Curtin. Professor Copland spruiked an egalitarian approach to wealth-creation which, quickly perused, could be construed as a local brand of socialism. Copland had consulted to governments for many years but he was no meek yes-man. His advice usually came unvarnished, as it did in his credo about post-war reconstruction:

It is not practicable, and it would not be progressive, to seek to return to an individual economy. What we should seek to secure is that those aspects of the productive economy which can no longer be individualist should not be in the control of private enterprise because they give a dangerous and anti-social opportunity for exploitation, and for the perpetuation of insecurity. They should be in the control of the whole community.[1]

Not really a Marxist decree, more a Keynesian parable of civic fellowship, Copland's essay urged legislators to invest in much the same *esprit de corps* that had distinguished Australian troops throughout World War II.

The communal spirit warming Copland's thinking was the distillation of a public mood. In the waning stages of the war, before the fighting corps had even been demobilised, many Australians were already nostalgic for troop allegiance. Throughout the long years of hostilities, a generation of men had found structure and focus in military platoons, and now many of these recruits felt oddly adrift when they imagined their campaign tapering toward peace. Similar emotions galvanised thousands of women who had excelled in new roles within the domestic workforce. Soon to be untethered now, all these men and women were tottering toward freedom, yearning for more of the military fellow-feeling that had emboldened them against the cruelties of the belligerent world.

This paradox, this weirdly discomfited mood of the victors, is the topic of the most arresting and affecting contribution in *Post-war Reconstruction in Australia*. It comes from H. C. 'Nugget' Coombs, who was then in the second year of his role as federal director-general of Post-war Reconstruction. In future decades Coombs would become the most influential and celebrated public servant in Australian history. Among his numerous achievements, he would become governor of the Reserve Bank, inaugural chairman of the Australia Council for the Arts and chairman of the Australian Council for Aboriginal Affairs. Repeatedly throughout his career Coombs would produce reports and memos that were exquisitely crafted to rouse prime ministers and cabinets into action. The documents in which he presented the case for the creation of the Australia Council for the Arts, for example, are now case studies in the generative possibilities of the best administrative prose.

In 1944 Coombs' star had only just begun to ascend, but even then he appeared fearless when speaking his truths to power. His chapter in *Post-war Reconstruction in Australia*, entitled 'The Economic Aftermath of War,' is not only an inventory of infrastructural imperatives. It is also a nuanced plea to invest in a salving and sentimental education for all the worn-out citizens in the nation.

In his essay Coombs wants economics to be neither dismal nor a science. 'The real test of the economic system,' he declares, 'is not the flow of goods and services it produces but the life which it makes possible for those who are dependent on it.'[2] His criteria of economics are phatic before they are mathematic: 'During the war, we have lived at an emotional pitch more intense than can be sustained for long periods.' He remembers that 'we were in the early stages called upon to face great dangers and to strain our capacities to the utmost'. Now he discerns 'some tendency for our concentration to slacken'. From this lassitude something poignant and perilous looms:

> There is a great danger that when the war itself is over we will be tired by the mental and spiritual strain of years

of war and will be unwilling to strive further. There is a danger that when we realise that the objectives for which this war has been fought have not been attained by the war itself, we will be disappointed and that when we realise that we have gained only the opportunity to work for these objectives, there will be disillusion and cynicism.[3]

With its echoed phrasing - 'There is a great danger…There is a danger…' - with the word 'war' murmured twice in each sentence, with the stretched single syllables of 'tired,' 'strive' and 'strain', with the menace and fuzzed sibilance of 'disillusion and cynicism', Coombs' stately paragraph blends his wide-awake intellect with emotions that you would expect in lyric verse rather than administrative discourse.

Indeed, Coombs writes with grace and gravitas matching a poetic exemplar from the same year: Kenneth Slessor's *Beach Burial*. Although Slessor depicts a more baleful scene, there is between him and Coombs a consonance of longing, a shared weary truth-telling and a staunch resolve to press on:

> Softly and humbly to the Gulf of Arabs
> The convoys of dead sailors come;
> At night they sway and wander in the waters far under,
> But morning rolls them in the foam.
>
> Between the sob and clubbing of gunfire
> Someone, it seems, has time for this,
> To pluck them from the shallows and bury them in
>   burrows
> And tread the sand upon their nakedness;

> And each cross, the driven stake of tidewood,
> Bears the last signature of men,
> Written with such perplexity, with such bewildered pity...[4]

In counterpoint but also attuned to the elegiac notes that toll in Slessor's writing, Coombs expresses his obligation not to the war-dead but to the survivors. He imagines how divorced from life the drifting homecomers must feel:

> More than 700,000 Service men and women and a similar number of war workers will at the end of the war find their occupations, which had given purpose to their lives for the past four years, no longer relevant.[5]

Envisaging this large fraction of the nation so bereft, Coombs wants a soulful civil service that can help the weary citizens toil through their dolours:

> New tasks with new social purposes must be found for them. They must adapt themselves to new environments, new sets of people. Many of them will have returned to domestic and personal relationships which have become strange and unreal. We must expect that in the post-war years there will be a strong element of instability in the psychological make-up of the people.[6]

I have read Coombs' essay many times since I first encountered it in undergraduate studies, almost four decades ago. It has always seemed remarkable, this policy document that is so tender-hearted at every point where you expect it to be hard-headed, with its compassion and its cadences giving lovely care to its prosody.

But not until I started a special research project did I grasp how uncannily revealing the essay is as a snapshot of its times.

In 1995 I began investigating an archive of forensic photography that is held by the Justice and Police Museum in Sydney. The collection covers police-work in the harbour city from the 1890s through to 1970, but the bulk of the material is from 1944 to 1960. In thousands of images, particularly in the files from just after the war, the town appears to be struggling with a collective concussion. There is almost no comfort on show. Streets are treeless, gardens are dilapidated, domestic and commercial interiors fret in Depression-era stasis. People crowd onto trams or trudge long treks to and from meagre employment, no matter whether they are crooks on the lurk or ordinary folks grubbing rent-money.

So high was the proportion of remarkable images in this archive, so aesthetically sophisticated and sociologically revealing were the photographs, I decided I had to talk with some of the men who produced them. These old chaps were not easy to find. Many had passed away. The few I tracked down were wary at first. Most were disinclined to replay the thirty or forty years they had spent stepping through blood, shit and petrol, but they were more than a little pleased that someone was interested in the work they had done. Eventually, I got to spend slow afternoons with a few of these careful men. Big pots of tea stewed on tables in sunrooms out back of modest beach houses dotted along the NSW Central Coast, where most of the detectives had retired with their pensions, a full six hour drive from the Big Smoke.

After a few interviews it became evident that these reserved old gents had decided to talk to me because it was a chance to spend time again telling stories. Yarning with me, or more precisely *at* me, the men evoked the gone camaraderie of the police force. Almost every one of them had come out of the military in

1945, adept at some technical task such as gunsight calibration or cartography or radar interpretation. As more than one of them said to me, verbatim, 'I hit civvy street looking for a job that would take care of me for life.' I remember a detective doodling on the lino with his walking stick while he reminisced, 'the fellas I knew who didn't go into the force: they became firemen, or ambulance drivers. Everyone wanted to be in some kind of troop.'

This sent me back to Coombs' essay, pondering that generation of homecoming men. My father's generation. I imagined the old coppers as youngsters working out how to make sense of their crime scenes, these new, civvy-street conflict-zones. The interviews helped me understand how the police force, the fire brigade and the ambulance corps offered comparatively benign versions of the military ordeal that these men already knew well. 'By joining the force,' one of the men confided, 'I could hunker down for the duration…Without too much uncertainty, I could wait out my days.'

That is what these squads of men did plenty of during and after the war: waiting.[7] My father used to say that the best way to understand his war experience was wrapped up in the wry order that he would hear several times a day: 'Hurry up and wait!'

What did men do in those times, when they were waiting? They told stories, to while away time. But also to wrap up advice and hard-won wisdom in a canny, roundabout delivery. Up in Queensland, for example, after recovering from his stint in the army, my father formed a small woodworking firm with a multicultural workforce never larger than a platoon. 'Smoko' breaks were sacrosanct at the workshop. Everyone would down tools, roll a cigarette or brew tea, and wait for someone to start yarning. Assayed as knowledge, a typical story by these fellas was not a bland set of instructions. Rather, most of their tales braided intrigue and wit till a moral emerged, while the listeners privately imagined themselves inside the scenes. By listening in on a story, you could get ready for the time when you would be caught in a comparable bind, and you could trust that one of the hundreds of yarns that you had heard had already paced you through the predicament. You could know your options, courtesy of all the listening and narrating you had done during all those past doldrums of waiting.

I knew from my father's tales that the storyteller occasionally tried for something more. More than just a gag or an axiom or a neat batch of information. I knew that my father and many of his workmates treasured the rare moment when the conditions were right to offer some version of a recalled event that had the quality of an epiphany. I recognised this precious genre from my father's repertoire. Sparingly offered, it was the laconic gift of a tale that grew more quiet and compelling till you realised you were getting something better than bullshit, some recounted experience that finished in a transcendent gleam. The special yarn was proof that you could spend at least some of your life on the far side of ordinary, out past the edges of the dull world of waiting. You could get away from the world that Coombs' essay lit up and loosened: the society he described as 'war-weary…and psychologically unstable'.[8]

I can finish my chapter with one of these special yarns. A detective gave me the story. As a parable it is a proper complement to Coombs' chapter of policy. It came when I asked him, 'How was it in the beginning, when you started taking the photos?'[9]

The old man hunched a moment, then he leaned forward to say that his first assignment was night-time out in a bushland suburb. Freezing cold. This was August 1946. A policeman had phoned, saying there'd been a knife fight in a fibro bungalow and the victim had been pursued onto the road, where he died after a bit more of a struggle. The detective rode his sidecar motorbike from the city to the scene. He came with a load of flash-powder canisters, because he expected there would be no electricity. Having worked with explosives during the war, he had an idea how he might generate light for his picture. When he pulled up at the scene, the local constable was waiting for him, pointing into gloom. The detective wrestled the bike around and kept it idling so the headlight threw a meagre beam toward the corpse. Taking care not to step into the surrounding evidence, the detective built a broad arc of connected flash canisters. He then rigged the camera on a tripod, and made ready to take the picture. When he touched a lit match to the short fuse, all the powder went up in a brilliant, cascading whoosh.

What happened next, he's never been able to figure whether it was because of the slight warmth still in the victim, or perhaps it was some freak effect of the breeze, or something spookier than that. Anyway when he clicked the camera just a heartbeat after the powder began to flare, he got a scalding vision of the body lying face-up to the sky as if it was floating a few inches from the ground, and hovering over the corpse there appeared a haze of steam or smoke or grey light that looked like a priest leaning over. Then darkness flooded back and he stood there in a blind dazzle while he listened to a crowd of people screaming and running, which he understood a few seconds later was in fact all the birds clearing out from the hundreds of trees around the scene. How weird. Those birds had been covertly watching him since he arrived. Almost no event goes without a witness.

Waiting a while longer for his sight to come back, smelling the cordite in the air, that is when he thought, 'This'll do me…I'll sign on for this.'

Notes

1. D. B. Copland, 'The Change-over to Peace', in D. A. S. Campbell (ed.) *Post-war Reconstruction in Australia*, Australasian Publishing Company, Sydney, 1944, p. 125.
2. H. C. Coombs, 'The Economic Aftermath of War' in D.A.S. Campbell (ed.) *Post-war Reconstruction in Australia*, Australasian Publishing Company, Sydney, 1944, p. 81.
3. Coombs, in Campbell, pp. 76–7.
4. K. Slessor, *Beach Burial*, written in 1944, in D. Haskell (ed.) *Kenneth Slessor: Poetry, essays, war despatches, war diaries, journalism, autobiographical material and letters*, University of Queensland Press, Brisbane, 1991, pp. 48–9.
5. Coombs, in Campbell, p. 77.
6. Coombs, in Campbell, p. 77.
7. There were, of course, women's versions of these wartime experiences. Coombs' essay spoke as much for the women as for the men. But my research has not led me to the women's experiences. They are a vital subject for another investigation.
8. Coombs, in Campbell, p. 78.
9. It was a condition of my research that all information, including the stories, should remain anonymous in perpetuity.

13

THE SEARCHERS DISMANTLED

Every now and then I delve into my files to puzzle over an essay called 'Sunspots', published by Fereydoun Hoveyda (1924–2006) in *Cahiers du cinéma* in 1960.[1] Each time, I marvel at how it is beautiful and strange, possibly meaningless, possibly brilliant. Mostly, 'Sunspots' describes the *dynamics*—the shifting rhythms, trajectories and perspectives dispersing you all over imaginary space—that you feel when attending the cinema.

Using images and ideas not customary in conventional European aesthetics, Hoveyda explains that cinema works best when it captures and channels an ever-unfolding force that runs through the represented spaces and temporal rhythms of a film and also through the audience in the dark auditorium. Energy pulses coherently in space, in time and in people so that the animus of the film flares through all the components of each individual shot and then arcs like electricity from shot to shot, from moment to moment, from screen to audience and back again. The rhythms and melody lines (visual as well as sonic) all generate a charge that carries, excites and transforms every part of the film, including the viewer, who is not separable from the luminous deluge. Characters, objects, spaces, luminance, time-patterns and viewers all get altered as the dynamics play out. The result is pantheistic somehow. When a film lights up like this, swirling around us and through us while activating everything

The Searchers Dismantled

that we can perceive, an intensified charge has been harnessed. In front of the cinema screen, we are sometimes bathed and buffeted by a force that is comprehensive and vital like the sun. Hence the name: 'Sunspots'.

When I first encountered Hoveyda's essay as a postgraduate philosophy student during the 1980s, I thought: 'Maybe it's a con: a parlour game staged by one of the *Cahiers du cinéma* insiders under cover of an extravagant *nom de plume*.' But I thought too that it had a palpable sincerity, that it was propelled by an ardent intellect and an avid emotion, that it fizzed with a yearning for the power that courses through movies. I sensed how the author revered radiance and really wanted to *know* kinetic urgency, to be true to the dynamics that define cinema. I remember thinking, 'Maybe it's some kind of mystical text a Sufi thing perhaps a sparkling mystery designed to riddle some realisation slowly out from my bewilderment'. That thought passed through me momentarily until, youngster that I was, I let some other notion take me elsewhere.

Even so, I have kept returning to 'Sunspots'. And I have learned a little about Hoveyda. I have learned that he was indeed a *Cahiers* editor, but not with a *nom de plume*. I have learned how he was the son of a diplomat and eventually became a celebrated philosopher, historian and metaphysician. So it is probably true that a kind of mysticism preoccupies him in his essay. (Whether this mysticism is 'sufi' at all, I am not qualified to say.) In the secular domain, he was appointed Iranian ambassador to the United Nations; and his older brother Amir Abbas Hoveyda was prime minister in the Shah's regime prior to being executed in 1979 during the fundamentalist revolution. When the younger Hoveyda wrote 'Sunspots', he was living in Paris, studying aesthetics and developing an enduring friendship and professional partnership with the great neo-realist director, Roberto Rossellini.

As for the elemental energies that Hoveyda brought so lucidly into focus, actually they have always been part of cinema. When the Lumière Brothers set up their first films in the 1890s, for example, viewers flocked to the screenings when they heard chattered reports of magical, animistic trees! Maxim Gorky was one reporter who was disturbed by the way some kind of ghost-power seemed to shiver the leaves of windblown foliage.[2] Framed aloft in the dark, the trees appeared to be oddly alive. For Gorky, cinema offered life in spectral form. He saw not an intensification or clarification, but a leached trace of natural vitality. It worried him. However, it galvanised him too; the vivacity in the prose of his accounts betrays this much. All those entities moving on the screen: they were like kindred creatures signalling to the human beings in the darkened room, as if the screen were transmitting a fellow-feeling that jumped out of the trees, across the auditorium, into the audience, and back again. In such a world, all things with movement in them might be considered siblings somehow. If city-folk had lost the ability to sense such animism, this cinematograph might bring the citizens back to the mysteries. Perhaps cinema, which Gorky called 'the kingdom of shadows', was too savage for him. Too pagan. But he could not stop himself confessing how engaging it was.

At cinema's inception, many people felt they had access to a quickened world: one they had lost in modernity but could recognise as kindred to them, perhaps in some ancestral way, as soon as they saw it jittering above and through them. Observing the moving pictures, viewers encountered an active world flaring out against darkness, a world where objects and matter were never dull or inert, a world that was protean therefore, spirited and wondrous, perhaps even sacred and subjectively driven. Cinema came as a cult for shape shifters, animated by that radiant energy which Hoveyda would later evoke so well in his metaphor of the transformative sunspot.

In recent times, the practice of ecology has helped us understand how an interconnecting energy might weave through space and time so that the definitions of what is inert and what is alive must be adjusted. Many cultures give spirit-names to an animating force that binds places, things and rhythms into the lively world. Hoveyda hinted at spiritualism when, like an astro physicist priest, he suggested that the cinema screen in the auditorium resembles the sun in deep space, its energy boiling on the surface and surging into the dark ambit, altering everything that has light in it or on it.

I've tarried awhile with Hoveyda because he can help sell my fundamental idea: that a film can generate in the viewer an invigorated *sense of self* that is also an energetic *sense of place*. Like some phosphorescent transformer exciting space with light and sound and time, a film can build up a luminous charge. Thus the cinema screen is no mere lodgement for the things represented on it; rather it is an energy field connecting the viewer to the cosmos, making a dynamic place in the continuously remembered time whereby the viewer gets meshed into all the delineated scenes of the film. Every thing activated on and by the screen gets transformed so that each thing represented there can no longer be known as a self-contained object but must be understood anew in every instant as a sensate and interconnected part of a flowing system of energy sizzling in space and time. This is a fact: the screen pulses with light and movement. Energy. And this energy moves through the viewer and then goes back to the world via the theatre where all the witnessing souls are not only transfixed but also galvanised by the imagery.

Irradiated thus, consciousness can alter and expand radically during a movie. I mean *all consciousness*—of the entire represented world, not just the viewer. The screen receives and generates energy over time. This energy affects every thing it plays upon, every thing represented on the screen and every thing in the auditorium and beyond. Such is the allure of cinema: it engrosses us in its forcefield; it helps us feel a volatile but coherent world surging through our nervous systems; it alters us at the core and at the edges of what we think to be our selves.

Which brings me, at last, to my exemplary energetic artefact, John Ford's Western, *The Searchers* (1956). Taking Hoveyda's ideas, sensing how they resonate with some other practical philosophies of place-enchantment and remembrance (for instance, the writing of David Mowaljarlai and Bernard Cache, both of whom have already featured significantly, along with Hoveyda, in previous chapters of this book), I will assay the extraordinary power in the opening minutes of Ford's masterpiece, to understand the way it remakes, remembers and *replaces* me, every time I become part of it.[3]

Here we are at the movies. Leave the workaday world in the foyer. Take a seat in the theatre. Now *The Searchers* starts by marking its own edge: the lights go down and in the darkness you get a symphonic blast from an orchestra, a couple of frames ahead of the Warner Bros logo. The noise and the logo set a boundary in time and space: 'for this session, your film consciousness starts here and now.' Next come the credits. And a song, intoning 'What makes a man to wander?' You're being eased out of the concerns that you brought into the auditorium. The song lulls and lets you loosen your focus, lets you wander just a little till the credits have done the business and the lyrics tail out: '*ride away… ride* away…ride away.'

Then blackness. Followed by a single white title on black: 'TEXAS 1868'.

And blackness returning, as the title fades off.

Fleetingly you realise that the sequence has taken on the rhythm of a person blinking.

Then, continuing that rhythm, a patch of whiteness intrudes on the blackness, and in the next blink you understand that you are seeing a door being unlatched like an opening eye. You are seeing from inside a dark room that looks out onto a landscape that is so bright and stark you cannot help but keep blinking.

In the door frame there is a woman, silhouetted like a dark pupil, who looks out from the room's eye. Then comes a tracking drift forward toward the door and across the threshold, out to the liminal porch while the woman moves as if she is being pulled by some motive stronger than the combined propulsion of her own walking and the implied push of the dollied camera. A startling play of forces contend at the door frame: wind ruffles her clothing; light pours in towards you; she stutter-steps forward; the camera half-follows-half-shoves her out to the porch until she and you sense that it is *the landscape* holding her now, more than equalling the power of the camera, momentarily. Indeed, the camera seems to acknowledge this—it stops its push forward, with the effect that after all this blinking, pulsing, breathy buffeting, pushing and pulling, after the mess of all this organic effort...everything pauses in a tense, elastic balance. She stops, and the camera stops as if it has surrendered, for now, to her will while she halts and looks out and the wind plays all over her edges, as if to signal that this stillness is not stoppage but just a moment in which restless movement changes rather than ceases.

Let's stop the film awhile. For we need to remember everything that has been implied in this initial shot.

After examining this sequence countless times over the years, I now understand that just about everything that will come in *The Searchers* has already been presaged in the first shot. The whole film is given to us not as a set of themes or meanings, but as a system of power surges back and forth between the incursive and the incumbent, between place and space, the built and the given, the imposed and the impounded, the past and the present poised to plunge into the future. Ford will spend the rest of the film teasing all this out as meaning. But in his first camera set-up, he gives us the entire movie as a retinue of contending *sensations*. He gives us an overwhelming sense of a place as a dynamic system charged by memory and desire.

When running the film in a dark lecture hall, I often call out to the room, asking students to ask themselves, 'Who or what is looking right now? Who or what is listening right now?' Also I ask, 'What forces are shaping the scene right now, what is making everything tend in a particular direction?' At first I have to badger the class, repeating the questions several times over. For it takes everyone a while to sense what we are looking for: we are trying to divine a kind of organised, shapeshifting spirit moving through the film and through ourselves.

'Who or what is looking right now?' 'Who or what is listening right now?' 'What forces are shaping the scene right now? What is making everything tend in a particular direction?' Let's go back and put these questions to the first shot of *The Searchers*.

Note how I kept talking about *the camera* following and looking? Well, that was me avoiding the most unsettling issue, which is…the camera is really just a device serving something else that's doing the looking. Yes, it is you—the viewer, served by the camera—doing the looking. *But it is something else too.* Already the film has turned you into something other than yourself. It is a sensation that is both unsettling and thrilling. By the end of the first shot, the viewer is you and something more than you. You sense it before you know it.

Who or what is looking and listening?

We will get to an answer before too long. But first let's just keep the question ticking over in the background while I set *The Searchers* running again.

The second shot of the film is a tight reverse-view. It lets you look at the woman and at the windowed wall of the cabin (this wall-eyed, wind-eyed cabin) behind her. On the steps of the porch, the camera is still attached to the cabin, you surmise, and the landscape is at your back, feeling ominously present behind you. So, from these steps on the porch, the camera looks at her looking. She is still buffeted by the wind and by the light and she holds on to a stanchion while she raises her left hand in a balancing gesture that also affords her some shade. She is awash in all kinds of energy. And some of it is tamped inside her, ready to pour out. You can see that.

Who or what is looking *right now*? Well, it is no human character that we have met. It is the film itself, possibly. But that is too glib. In this shot offered from the steps, the looking thing—the conscious thing—is rhythmically related to whatever was looking in the first shot. I feel this relationship because of a continuity that flows across the edit from the first shot to the second. This continuity, which has been sustained by the music and the wind, tells me that the entity looking is the same in each shot, despite the radically different perspectives availed by the camera. This entity is extensive, large and contains multitudes.

Then comes the third shot, from a new place on the porch. Looking out toward the sunlight, we get a full view of a landscape with a horseman approaching in the middle distance. We see how the wind keeps agitating. We see the wind working on a blanket slung across a tethering rail that marks the edge of the cabin in the lower foreground.

With the next camera-shift, looking back to the cabin, from the steps again, we see people start to come out of the front room, as if drawn out by the landscape but also as if wilfully disgorged by the cabin. Something palpable pushes out from the cabin and through you as you feel yourself placed between the forces defining the cabin and the forces defining the landscape. These contending dynamics move you and move through you. As this feeling registers, three more people ooze out from the cabin. A dog comes out too, onto the porch. Then another person. It is as if the cabin has chosen to produce all these emissaries in response to the stimulus of the landscape and the horseman. The dog starts barking. You realise that you are *listening* (and thus placing yourself aurally) while you are *looking,* and because sound is so much more surrounding and immersive than perspectival vision, you realise that the soundtrack has been 'dispersing' you all over the scenes from the first instant the film commenced.

Still on the porch, but from an entirely new camera set-up now, you get a mid-shot view of the dog. Then with the sound of the dog still barking, you get a view which might be from the perspective of the dog, but it might also be from any or all of the human characters who have been spirited out of the cabin. And from this camera-vantage, you see that John Wayne has brought his outrider character, Ethan, to the steps of the porch.

You see looks and handshakes exchanged. You hear choppy noises of greeting and waiting. All this is perceived from camera set-ups on the porch and from a 'hearing place' that is nowhere pinned down: that is everywhere.

Then there is a wide shot, from out in the landscape, looking back to the cabin from the 'wild' side of the tethering rail. You feel this cut like something shocking, thrilling and threatening. It is a major development. For the first time, you are clearly detached from the cabin, and it feels hugely significant, panicky in its importance. This sense of panic flickers half-formed in you, before the camera bumps you back to the more comforting porch-step position and frames a close view of the cabin. You thank the film for this return of sanctuary. Oddly, you feel you have come back to yourself, you have remembered yourself.

Next, from the porch steps, you see and *feel* a sequence that is flat-out astonishing. As the woman keeps her eyes on Ethan, she backs into the cabin, through the door and into its interior. Ethan moves forward, as if drawn by powers stronger than him. And everyone else, including the dog, does the same. Ineluctably, it seems, the cabin takes everyone into itself.

To show this ingestion, the camera has rebounded, with a hard cut, back out into the country. From out on the wild edge of the landscape, out where you have just had that sudden feeling of disturbing detachment, you see the cabin reclaim its settlers and you feel how keen you are to be drawn back in there too. You feel it like an organic flex in yourself, as if you are craving to be part of the cabin, as if you have rights and responsibilities over every thing in the cabin. Now that this intruder Ethan has come into the world and now that the film has buffeted your edges, you feel a need to find yourself again. And you realise, with a shock that is vertiginous and *organic*...you realise that you have become the cabin!

The cabin is yourself! All the camera set-ups and edits have built and braced you so. And it is a living thing, this cabin. It is the eye of this desert world. It is the sensate centre. It is pulsing, blinking, looking, listening, remembering. The cabin has worldly compulsions coursing through it. It is no inert object. It is assertive. It is a being in a large system of needing and wanting. You know this because you have felt what it feels, and you have felt your need for it. You have experienced a spirit-possession of sorts. You have been mildly inculcated to an animistic realm, a world where every thing is live and conscious. (Remember Gorky's astonishment in front of the shivering trees.)

Question: Who or what is looking, listening, breathing, feeling? Answer: For the first five minutes or so, it is the cabin. It is you as the cabin, as this conscious space. This realisation finishes the film's prelude.

Next there is a lengthy interior sequence where you understand evermore clearly that if the cabin walls could speak they would tell of a painful and only partially acknowledged yearning between Ethan and the woman. Only three characters know this completely: the woman, Ethan and the cabin. How achingly the cabin knows it. How nobly the cabin keeps its knowledge. Indeed, how nobly the cabin does its myriad different keeping tasks. It keeps coolness and shaded ease safe against the hot glare of the landscape; it keeps a spectrum of colours in balance—blues against reds—as it arrays a comforting space for all these folks surviving not only the abrasions of the landscape but also (we glean this knowledge from conversations) the recent depredations of the Civil War. The cabin keeps domestic stillness counterpoised against natural wildness and political malfeasance. The cabin knows everything that has passed amongst this tiny, vulnerable colony. And you are beginning to know this too, because you have been allowed to be the cabin. You don't know it *cerebrally* so much as *nervously*, as a series of blinking, pulsing emotions, anxieties and affections all infused within the cabin. You feel a real affection—self-love I suppose it is—for the timber and stone, for the table, the crockery, the stove, for the spaces of conviviality that the cabin offers to all the desiring characters who are sluicing around inside it. You feel the cabin's organic completeness, its sensitivity.

This is why you will feel something like a nervous collapse at the first narrative turning-point, a few minutes later, when the cabin and most of its humans are destroyed by the Comanche raid.

Inveterate *Searchers* watcher that I am, each time I witness the raid I feel the desecration of the cabin with an electrical distress that takes charge of me and commands my allegiance, for a while, to the berserker vengeance of Ethan. The nervous shock I feel when the cabin gets destroyed impels me into the film, compels me to ride alongside Ethan in shock and with my blood up, accompanying the mad revenger until I come to my senses anew and realise finally, sixty minutes later, that he is insane and inhuman and I have to find or *make* another consciousness that can lead me to another morality—not Comanche and not Ethan – that might guide me through the tragedy of this stolen country. Over the duration of the entire film I experience an ethical flow from naïve affection, to blood-simple revenge, to analytical reflection, to personal conjecture, innovation and conviction.

This is the greatness of *The Searchers*: it is an active and activating system of urges all organised toward the creation of an ethical system which is not clearly modelled at the start. The film just propels me toward this unguided place. There is no point of moral stasis (other than Ford's overwhelming affirmation of the basic goodness of generous love, perhaps) pinning the film down, treatise-like. I am not propelled toward one unarguable standpoint. Rather, the film puts me in motion, tipping me into its moral turbulence and setting my passions in contention with my reason.

Over a couple of hours, the film lets me know space and time that are neither 'Western' nor 'indigenous', that are both animistic and objective, that are ancient and entirely contemporary and always under construction. The film makes a moral landscape that is restless but coherent.

All the transformations that the film works on you, they push you toward new knowledge. But it is a knowledge that looms in your sentiments before it registers in your intellect. Only afterwards as the end credits roll, when you're enthralled, puzzled and reflective, only then can you bring some of these sensations into cognition. This is not to say the film is 'savage' or 'primitive' particularly, but it is certainly not Cartesian!

Which brings me back to the philosophies of place that I have been reading while getting ready to display my *Searchers* mania in public like this.

Perhaps the most 'visionary' of these philosophies comes from David Mowaljarlai, an Indigenous Australian Elder who spent the final twenty years of his life creating a spiritual system—pragmatic, ethical, ecological—that he was determined to communicate to non-Indigenous Australians. This system was based on ritual knowledge stored in his country in the northwest of the continent and it was enlivened by his bold decision to share portions of this knowledge more broadly than they had ever been transmitted before. Reasoning that the colonial invasions have brought so much fundamental change that the Indigenous systems need to react by changing too, Mowajarlai asserted that the country has psychic, social, geological and botanical life all synthesised into a vitality that can guide a person to sensible actions. Strictly, literally *sensible*.

In the writings and interviews that he left as a deliberate legacy, Mowaljarlai describes how he can feel the presence (or not), the valence (or not), the direction (or dissipation) of this vitality and how he can act in communion with it. It is an erotics of country, a system of compulsions, sacred but also mundane and practical. Mowaljarlai can find spots in space and moments in time where the urgency in country is intensified, where this force signals through to the inhabitants most emphatically. He says he can sense the land's animus 'swinging' around him.[4] He can attune to it through cultural work, through ritual tale-telling and remembering, making events and structures that frame and intensify the force—marking the ground, lodging painted figures in caves, determining sightlines to other sacred zones, bouncing sound off cliff faces. In other words, he arranges a mise en scène of country and from that mise en scène he gets cues for action, taking direction from the scene, on the understanding that countless ancestors have already fashioned it, through communal memory-keeping, into a kind of energy-generator and view-finder.

Mowaljarlai and Hoveyda would have understood portions of each other's beliefs. As would Bernard Cache when he describes how architecture is a managed confluence of space and time best understood as 'a cinema of things', a system of frames and folds which channel the continuous flow of matter and moments through each other, integrating all the substances, surfaces, sheets of light, vaults of air and volumes of sound that are ready to resonate in any environment.[5]

Here it is useful to reprise the thoughts of Elizabeth Grosz, as I offered them in a previous chapter. Amplifying Cache's provocations, Grosz has suggested that architecture is place-making, and place-making is truly the primary art because it establishes frames that concentrate nature's dynamics—the sill of a door that makes a floor distinct from the ground, the soffit that emphasises the shelter of a roof against a wall, the frame forming a window, a directional cairn of stones that has been set down to show how to bring a river to you when you make tracks through a savannah. Grosz describes architecture as a place-making process whereby one renders space *lively* by harnessing and organising the tendencies that are abroad in the territory that is being constructed.[6] Place-making does for space what social history and personal memory do for time—providing gravitas and momentum. It is close to Hoveyda's vision of cinema's irradiated universe.

So, to sum up and to lead you back to the film: the pulse detected by Mowaljarlai, Cache and Grosz accords with the liveliness you feel when you are the cabin in *The Searchers*.

As I have already observed in an earlier chapter, Dylan Thomas once wrote of his yearning to catch 'the force that through the green fuse drives the flower'.[7] The wonderful image bears reprising. For it feels *almost* right for what John Ford marshals in *The Searchers*, except that we need a metaphor with more heat in it, more blood. The cabin represents passion, even gore. It is more than a fuse. It is perhaps a beating heart, incarnadine. The cabin stands for colonialism and the clash between incursive and indigenous consciousness; it hosts domestic peace but it also shelters the hunter who has come home steeped in a carrion smell and unspeakable memories. In the cabin, femininity contends with masculinity and desire pushes against repression; passion disturbs reason and conciliation vies with vengeance. All these forces give a restive vitality to the cabin and make it a world animated with desire and history.

Ten minutes into *The Searchers*, because of the way the cabin has moved through you and made you as you have felt the flowing construction of the film, and because the cabin is the first creature killed in the film, you know in your nerves the drama of America, founded as it is on violence and landgrabbing, maintained as it is in spilled blood, burned as it is by all the flaring energy that drives it, inside and out, across all its spaces all through modern time. You understand that this is what *The Searchers* lets you feel: America and its place in the world, America and its place in and as yourself.

The cabin is you and the cabin is America. The nineteenth century. The twentieth century. The twenty-first. The beast itself, through all these times. America pulsing, America breathing, wanting, vulnerable as it is vital, mad as it is visionary. America in 1956, and remembered before then, and forever after. This made place, America. Always poised to be dismembered and dismantled even as it gets created, even as it remakes and replaces everyone who encounters it. Movie-made America. Remaking the entire world in its own image even as it remembers and makes its own place in the world.

Note: a different, animated version of this chapter first appeared in issue 8 of the splendid online journal, *Rouge* (www.rouge.com.au). I thank the editors for prompting me to work on these ideas and for giving the piece its first airing.

Notes

1 See *Cahiers du cinéma : 1960–1968—new wave, new cinema, re-evaluating Hollywood,* J. Hillier (ed.), Harvard University Press, Cambridge, MA, 1986.
2 M. Gorky, 'Newspaper review of the Lumiere programme at the Nizhni-Novgorod fair, *Nizhegorodski listok,* 4 July 1896', anthologised in C. Harding and S. Popple (eds), *In the Kingdom of Shadows: a companion to early cinema,* Cygnus Arts, London, 1996, pp. 5–6.
3 See D. Mowaljarlai and J. Malnic, *Yorro Yorro: everything standing up alive,* Magabala Books, Broome, 1993. See also B. Cache, *Earth Moves: the furnishing of territories,* MIT Press, Boston, 1995.
4 See D. Mowaljarlai, ABC Radio Feature, http://www.abc.net.au/rn/talks/8.30/lawrpt/lstories/lr311001.htm.

5 See particularly p. 29 and chapter 9, 'Oscillation' of Cache, *Earth Moves*.
6 See E. Grosz, 'Chaos, Territory, Art, Deleuze and the framing of the earth', in *IDEA Journal 2005*, S. Attiwill and G. Lee (eds), Brisbane, 2005, pp. 15–25.
7 D. Thomas, 'The Force that through the Green Fuse Drives the Flower', first published 1934, in D. Thomas, *Collected Poems 1934–1952*, Dent, London, 1966.

14

'WHO KNOWS THE WEATHER?' —THE MEMORY OF GREG DENING

I was invited to deliver the 2014 Greg Dening Memorial Lecture at the University of Melbourne. From the outset, protocol demanded that I offer a litany of thanks. There was a ceremonial aspect to these expressions of gratitude and debt: a ceremonial aspect that I take seriously. For the invitation was a great honour. And I felt obliged and benignly indebted to many people in a context so richly defined by the late and revered Professor Dening.

I expressed my indebtedness to:

Indigenous provenance, right up to the present moment.

I expressed my indebtedness to:

Joy Damousi and Ron Adams and everyone else associated with organising this important annual lecture.

Also to:

Donna Dening, for her work, her friendship and the inspiration she has long provided.

As well as to:

The Teasdale family of the Wimmera District in northern Victoria, whose archive of films I will be using as exemplary material throughout this essayistic rendition of the lecture.

And to:

My collaborators on the Teasdale work—Malcolm McKinnon, Ben Speth, Annie Venables, Acey Teasdale and Chris Abrahams.

Finally of course, I celebrated being immeasurably indebted to Greg Dening, whose brilliance and guidance continue unabated.

I emphasise that this account of debt and obligation is not *only* ceremonial. It is also *thematic*. This idea of mutual obligation is one of the main topics for this chapter. I want to understand better how we are indebted to others for our knowledge; how all utterances made in the present moment owe their existence and impact to work done by others in the past, no matter if this past is recent or ancient.

For greater precision, I use a term that Greg used often: we are all 'bound-together' in mutual obligation. Subjects, objects, agents, apparatchiks—past and present—we are all bound-together in a quest to understand the larger world that encompasses everyone drawing from and acting upon each other. Everyone. Every entity. Animal, vegetable and mineral. Past and present. Here and there.

Defining *connectedness*, I contend that historical understanding is the quest to grasp how anyone's present experience is dynamically and bewilderingly related to everyone else's past experience. *Connectedness*. Bound-togetherness. Or to borrow language from

'Who Knows the Weather?'

Greg again: 'Historical understanding is an overlaying of images one on the other…it is cumulative and kaleidoscopic'.[1]

Extrapolating from this fundamental idea of Greg's, and enriching the thematic promise of my chapter here, I can offer a list of cardinal notions that will guide my prose. I think of these cardinal notions as the 'Greg Dening Precepts', even though I know how wary Greg would have been not only of that word 'cardinal' but also of any suggestion that his precepts might set a *template* or a rigid model for thinking.

Anyway, here are the 'Greg Dening Precepts', which we will appreciate and utilise as we go:

> We need to live by the constant possibility that the past will surprise us.
>
> The making of histories is an 'unclosed action'. Our assertions and our understandings of the past are never settled.
>
> The making of histories is an imaginative act. And imagination is not fantasy. Imagination is: finding a word that others will hear…seeing what is absent… hearing the silence as well as the noise. Imagination is reading and writing with the whole body and all its emotions, not just with the mind.
>
> We never learn truths by being told them. We learn truths by experiencing them in some way.
>
> We do this work in order to change the world in some way, to shake its lethargy, to disturb its bad faith.

These precepts are drawn mostly verbatim from one of Greg's last published essays, titled 'Performing Cross-Culturally'.[2] That essay is a great summary work, a kind of credo, and I recommend it enthusiastically, especially for its emphasis on the generative, performative work that one must do at that edge where the cultures of the past and the present mesh and mash. I recommend the essay for the way it stresses that wonderment, curiosity and startling questions, not conclusive assertions, are the most important historical quarries. This is the cheering message that I take from all of Greg's work. I feel endorsed by him to concentrate on asking: 'What does the evidence make me *wonder*? What shift in my understanding, in my quests for knowledge, can I sense in the experience of encountering the liveliness issuing from the past?'

To thicken our thinking, I would like to supplement my selected 'Greg Dening Precepts' with an epigraph, whose theme will return at the end of the lecture. The epigraph, from the art historian Oleg Grober, need not make sense straight away. But it ought to mean something by the end of my talk:

> There is a discourse about the arts, rarely written and at times unspoken, which is neither that of historians so deeply tied to time and space nor that of critics concentrating on…contemporary judgements about whatever it is that they see. It is the discourse of sensibilities affected by the excitement of…impressions, it is a discourse of love.[3]

I want to take seriously this idea that there must be artistry in our work and that *love*—a particular experience of self-altering intensity—is inherent to the work. Love of the world. Love of experience. Love of the entities in the past and present to whom, to quote Greg again, we 'owe the dignity of being able to be themselves in our representations of them'.

'Who Knows the Weather?'

So, thus far in this chapter, we have had a ceremonial prelude, which has become a thematic declaration glossed by an epigraph that is tinted with romance.

Now I offer an overture, which I hope will take us into a symphony of ideas inspired by Greg.

I was asked to talk about some of my projects in a way that enhances an understanding of Greg Dening's lifelong project. I am thrilled to do this. I will talk about some work that a team of us—Malcolm, Ben, Annie, Chris, Acey, whom I have mentioned already—are doing with an archive of films and videos that have been recorded by three generations of the Teasdale family, on their farm at Rupanyup in the Wimmera. This wonderful archive starts with the films made by Relvy Teasdale before World War II, enriched prodigiously by several decades of superb film-making by Relvy's son, the late John Teasdale, from the 1950s onwards, and maintained nowadays by John's wife Dawn and their children and in-laws. (I should mention that a small but alluring portion of the archive is already available online, through the 'Culture Victoria' website of the State Government of Victoria: http://www.cv.vic.gov.au/stories/creative-life/john-teasdale-chronicle-of-a-country-life/. I should mention too that, outside the family itself, Malcolm McKinnon has performed the bulk of preparatory and institutional work to amalgamate, conserve and interpret the Teasdale archive.)

Now, because we are all bound-together with others who have represented the Wimmera already, the Teasdale archive resonates with previous renditions of that tract of country. In this instance tonight, in this overture, I will call on the poet John Shaw Neilson, who lived and worked and sang around and about this country at the start of the twentieth century.

Here then, in a bound-together or 'montaged' account, is a way to begin to be surprised by the records. Here is my overture introducing you to the Wimmera via some frame-grabs from the Teasdale archive embroidered, in the indented passage, with verbal evocations, or commentary, harvested from John Shaw Neilson's poems.

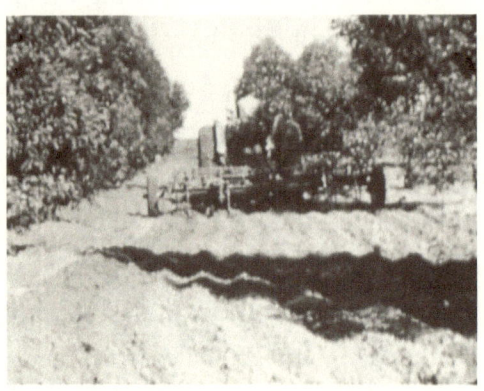

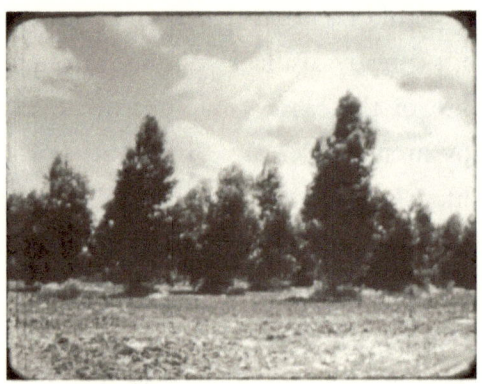

'Who Knows the Weather?'

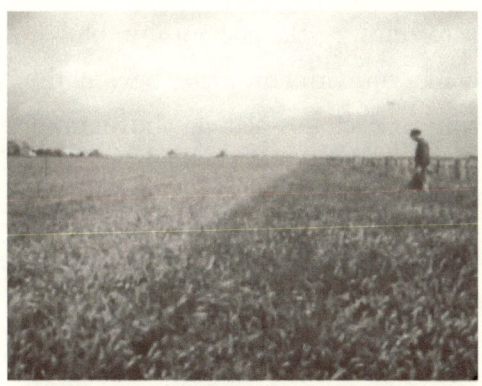

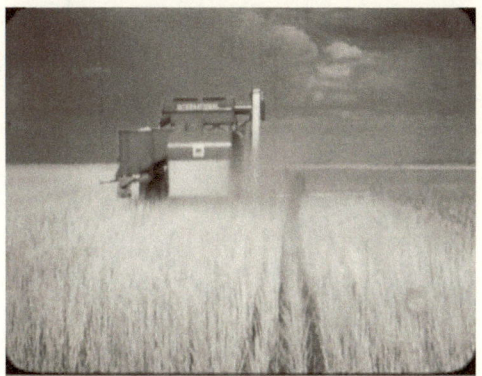

The Wimmera is a place defined, for a large portion of the year, by a dry and dispiriting heat. The tough summer wanes more slowly here than in most other parts of the land.

In the Wimmera, 'a cool wind must wait patiently for all the sun's delaying'. The people yearn toward the horizon-lands where 'the far sky [is] wonderful and dim'. Exhausted farmers crave 'the grey of even-time' and hanker for 'the cool earth and a sky delight-some mild'.

In the Wimmera, the late autumn bluster means 'the sky comes up with chronicles beyond the blue air blowing' and 'clouds play up above' until winter comes.

And as for the winter: it is bleak and buffeting, and the trees spend entire months dancing in 'white weather' unabated.

This gives you a sense of some *places* in the Wimmera. Additionally, John Shaw Neilson and John Teasdale studied people too…they studied the *faces* as well as the places of the Wimmera.

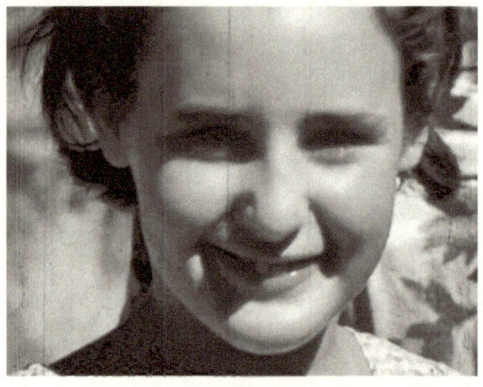

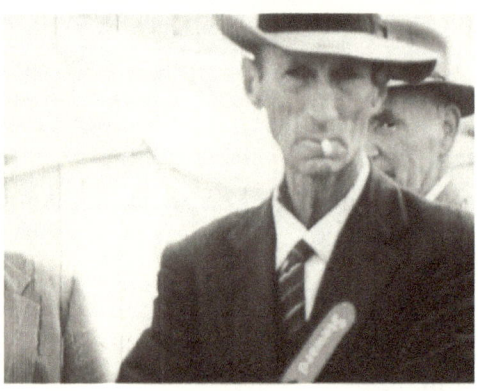

'Who Knows the Weather?'

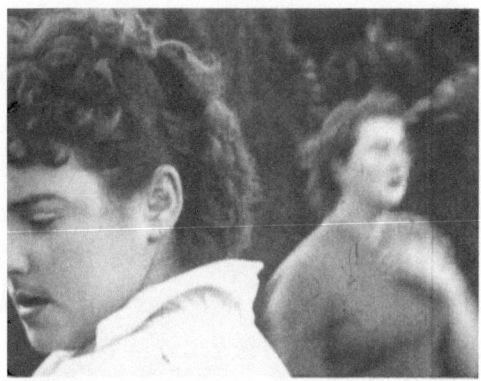

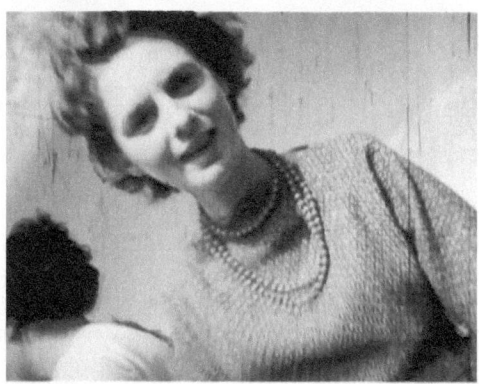

For example, to accompany some portraiture from John Teasdale's farming community, as shown above, here is Neilson's short poem, entitled Greeting:

> Fill up! Fill up! Today we meet:
> What of the wind? Who knows the weather?
>
> Shall we be old men in the street?
> What of the wind? Who knows the weather?
>
> Fill up! Fill up! Today we meet!

I mentioned the theme of *connectedness* a moment ago. It is everywhere in the Teasdale footage. Connectedness. Again and again, John Teasdale makes manifest his urge to show how someone or something connects to someone or something else. Imaginatively, John Teasdale finds the means—often via the manner with which he pans from one thing to another, or via the relationships amongst people and between people and things as they are put on display within a camera-frame from foreground to background—he finds the means to help you *know* this connectivity '*by experiencing it in some way*'.

In the autobiography by the great Dutch documentary filmmaker Joris Ivens, there is an illuminating passage where he recounts his experience working on a project about cooperative farming in Revolutionary Russia. Ivens describes how it took him several weeks in the field to understand how to convey the physical and cognitive duress that the workers were undergoing. Ivens explains that he learned slowly that it was not enough simply to record, at a discreet distance, the scenes and actions of the work squads. Instead he needed to find camera techniques, perspectives, rhythms and choreographies that helped the viewers *feel* in their nervous systems, in their musculature and in the flux of their moods…to feel the work and to feel the transformations that were being wrought by the work. So Ivens developed a 'vocabulary' of camera placements, perspectives, camera moves and shot durations that helped the viewer know, for example, the back pain, the thirst and wilful endurance associated with forest-clearing or crop-planting. Ivens was seeking the *cinematic* equivalent of what Greg Dening sought when looking for the right word or phrase that could shift the reader into knowing a truth 'by experiencing it in some way'.

'Who Knows the Weather?'

John Teasdale did the same. For example there is a marvellous sequence covering grain harvesting and bagging in the late 1960s.

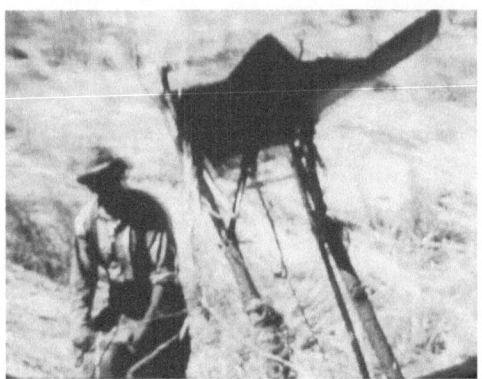

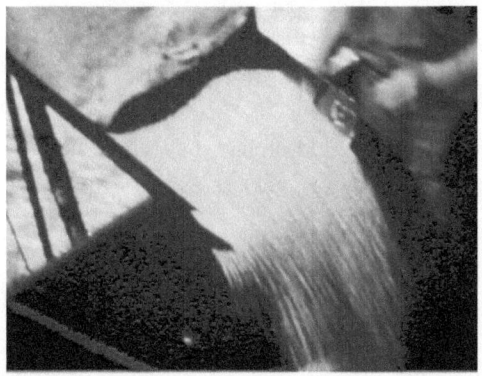

Watching these images, you can sense the thirst, the dryness, the noise, the repetitive, back-paining labour; you can know something that feels like truth about the duress of dry-country farming and the sense of unstinting commitment required to maintain that culture of work in the place, generation after generation.

As I say, I think Relvy and John Teasdale's cinematography chimes with Greg Dening's determination to 'find the right word', to imagine the expression that gives the experience of a shift in understanding. To do something more than 'bearing witness'. To bring revelation and move it through you.

Or to borrow from another fine mind whom I find increasingly instructive—namely the classicist and poet Anne Carson—we are always seeking expressive modes that perform something similar to what great drama can do. To quote Carson: '[effective dramatic staging] is simply a mirroring of the activity of the thought that you had at the time that you had it…[it is] an attempt to make that activity happen again in the mind [of the reader or the viewer].'[4]

And here I think of Greg Dening again, of an assertion I heard him say often in the intellectual 'retreats' (entitled 'Challenges to Perform') that he and Donna Dening convened at ANU throughout the late 1990s and early 2000s: he would say that the best writing enlivens your mind while the words are unfurling, till you arrive at the sudden moment where you pause reading, look up and are moved to exclaim, 'I was about to think that!' Once again: truth *experienced* rather than merely *told*.

With their intimate grasp of farmers' experience, the Teasdale films are deeply engaged like Greg's writing. Indeed, also like much of Greg's writing, the Teasdale films are *devotional*, I think. Devotional in their attentiveness to everyday experience in an agricultural community. And the main, knowledge-shifting force in the films is the way they grant us access to a suffusing, integrative urge—both social and natural—an urge that has enabled generations of settlers to apply themselves continuously to the task of teaching each other how to prevail in this place which is actually not especially congenial to farming economies.

What is this animus that I sense in the Teasdale films? It is a suffusing, integrative force encouraging rituals of attentiveness and education that help the filmmakers and the audience catch and convey knowledge intensified with a sense of allegiance. This knowledge flows through and out of the films, binding person to person to country in the Wimmera district, generation to generation. The knowledge connects people and places. It is knowledge about society and nature. It is a force that involves *information*, surely; but it also involves *affection* or powerful, animating emotions. Or to commandeer Raymond Williams' famous phrase, it is a force that sets up and derives from the 'structure of feeling' that holds a culture together over generations.[5]

In fact, having used this famous quote to cinch my point, I want to discard it immediately and replace it with a better but less-celebrated phrase from Raymond Williams. For cultures are more than *structural*; they are *systematic*. Williams came to understand this. Structures are too solid, too modelled. Instead, Williams changed his focus over time, to look for something definitive in all cultures, something he called 'social experiences in solution'.[6]

The phrase 'social experiences in solution' describes a flowing, suffusing predisposition in a culture, a *seeking* urge to fuse people to places through rituals and aesthetic artefacts, an urge that is much more slippery than a structured feeling. For a solution seeps and subtly transforms itself at the same time as it alters environing matters. Within the Teasdale footage this solution is a kind of passion—something insistent that agitates all the time it prevails. It is emotional—something that *moves*. It is a yearning for generational continuity. It is a love of the world binding together all its immersed and interconnected inhabitants.

To exemplify this notion, there are a some clips in the Teasdale collection, where John's voice can be heard speaking a commentary—truly he is *chanting* the commentary—naming places and people relative to one another as he pans around landscapes and ceremonies. John leans toward the microphone and intones quietly but with utter authority:

> This is John Teasdale speaking. And I'm going to voice-over some of these old films…This is down behind the dam, taken from the dam-bank…you see Old Ned's place over there…part of the Old Place away down there…Frank Childs's place…and straight down south is Cootes's…where Jimmy Coote used to live…there's the Black Range down there…Stawell…and as we come around you can see the Grampians coming into view… that's a little 17-acre paddock divided by a channel…a combination-drain down there that fills other peoples' dams…and we're panning now over where Clarrie Sheridan lived…

With this enchantment he is activating 'social experience in solution'. He is soaking the country in the extensive, seeping influence of the exactly identified people who have been devoted to specific plots of country distributed around the horizon-bound Wimmera plains. From the standpoint of the community that he knows and serves, John is *binding particular people to particular places*.

I am struck by the similarity between such sequences and scenes described by Eric Michaels in his studies of Central Australian Warlpiri Media videos, particularly the ground-breaking work of Francis Jupurrurla Kelly, where the sequence and tempo for panning the camera across country are governed by rules requiring the acknowledgement of ancestors and present custodians.[7] And while I know how easy it is to mistake mere correlation for real connection, I do think there is something striking in the way John Teasdale attends to generational husbandry and place-based responsibility in ways that are similar in their efficacy to the Indigenous systems. As we see again and again in rural Australia, there is a seepage between Indigenous and incursive cultures that manifests in myriad ways, not all of them benign of course; but not all of them simply malign either.

Which brings the right moment to consider the glimmers of Indigenous presence in the Teasdale archive. First point: they are the merest glimmers. But still they are discernible in this folk-ethnography devoted to settler culture. There are shots of Aboriginal men in crowd scenes and in aesthetically thrilling footage recorded at local football matches. There are shots of a handsome young black man working in a mechanics shop. Each black figure is always isolated, never surrounded by black *compadres*. But, as is always the way with John Teasdale's portrait footage, these men appear comfortable, poised, suffering no evident indignity, receiving unequivocal respect during the moments John focused on them.

These glimmers hold open an archive that, because of John Teasdale's universally attested integrity, cannot help but be candid. It is indeed an archive that manages, with its glimmers, to show absences and hear silences.

In a parallel way, this was always a compelling concern for Greg Dening (who was similarly routinely characterised as the embodiment of respect and integrity). In doing his history, Greg always tried to set the conditions for the seeping-in and amplification of voices that have not been terminally silenced. Or, to paraphrase what he often proclaimed: we must make sure that we mute no other voices by expressing our own. We must set the conditions for amplifying other voices without ventriloquising them.

As I have worked with the people working on the Teasdale footage, it has become clear that the films are animated by an open-ness to sensation and sensemaking; they are enlivened by a spirit of *commitment* to everyday experience that is more inclusive than exclusive of 'outsiders'. And with that spirit almost always luminous in the footage, working with the team of artists and scholars to bring the archive into popular awareness, we have been able to initiate consultations that have brought Indigenous voices and testimonies into dialogue with the Teasdale archive. Here in the settler–farmer community is Indigeneity—albeit glimpsed barely in passing—shown and held open as a portal to cause future, further testimony, further curiosity, further learning.

There is another batch of footage featuring John Teasdale's voice. The voice-over, in John's distinctive, quietly authoritative 'chant', bears witness this time to a connective urge seeping not from *place to people*, but from *people to people*:

> Now we're at the Rupanyup Show…There's Joan Newitt there…Beverly Morgan…Wendy Sprague and Norma Chapman there with the glasses on…Wendy has a look at the camera…'Yes, it is running'…Bernie Rooney… aaaah…Ned Valentine, I think…That's Gwenda Johnson…Pat Sheridan and her sister, I think…Barbara Nunn…Wendy Sprague and Norma Chapman…Old Hughie Mathewson…Reg Jackson…Dick Dunn!

I am struck, in this sequence, by the genealogical incantation that John Teasdale performs. Such name-listing is a practice of memorial, inter-generational binding that governs the memory-keeping of cultures—especially Indigenous cultures—all around the world, all through the ages.

There is real value in dwelling on John Teasdale's portraiture a while. Here are some more frames from sequences that are

'Who Knows the Weather?'

as attentive as anything I've seen anywhere in the international genre of intimate ethnography.

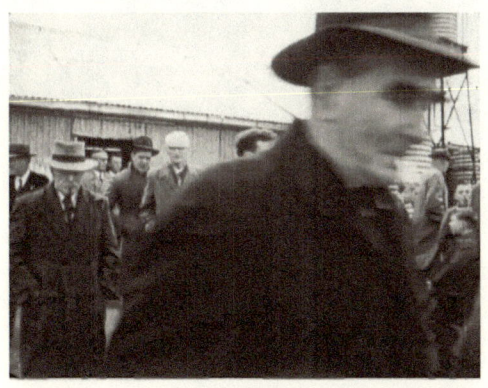

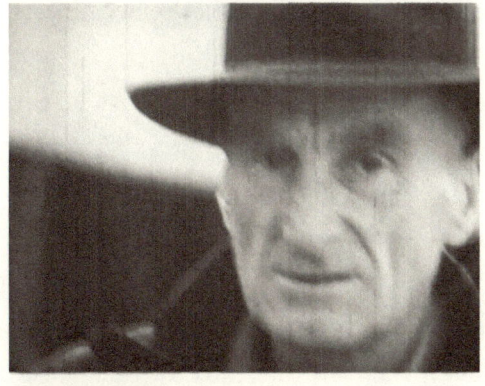

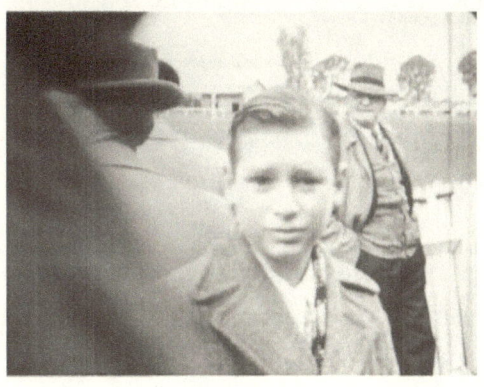

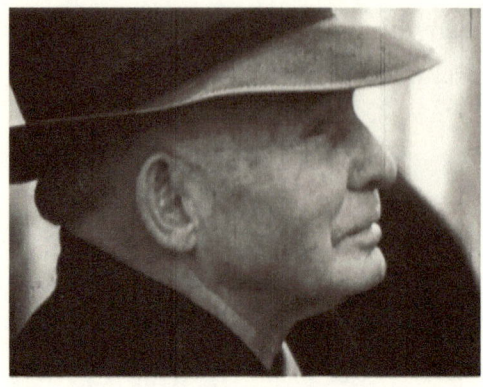

Looking at this footage, I sense the candour and respect that flows in both directions between John Teasdale and his subjects. (Note how the people appear as subjects, not objects; unvarnished, directly observed, never sentimentalised or criticised.)

And I am reminded of a befuddling and thrilling passage from one of the all-time great exemplars of intimate ethnography, James Agee and Walker Evans's *Let Us Now Praise Famous Men*. About a quarter of the way through the book, Agee pauses to wonder what he is doing with and to the sharecropper families who have become the focus of his fascinations after he has taken up residency with them in the midst of their unstinting poverty. Each time he looks at a sharecropper, he reminds himself:

> Here at the center is a creature: it would be our business to show how through every instant of every day of every year of his existence alive he is from all sides streamed inward upon, bombarded, pierced, destroyed by that enormous sleeting of all objects forms and ghosts how great how small no matter, which surround and whom his sense take: in as great and perfect and exact particularity as we can name them.

'Who Knows the Weather?'

> This would be our business, to show them each thus transfixed as between the stars' trillions of javelins and of each the transfixions: but it is beyond my human power to do so. The most I can do—the most I can hope to do—is to make a number of physical entities as plain and visible as possible and to make a few guesses, a few conjectures; and to leave to you much of the burden of realizing in each of them what I have wanted to make clear of them as a whole: how each is itself; and how each is a shapener.[8]

'Shapener' is not really a word. But it ought to be. I think it means 'someone who simultaneously shapes and is shaped by the external forces of the world'. Someone who alters when encountering an other. Someone who is simultaneously subject and object. A form-giver who is also a form-receiver.

I am reminded of one of my favourite English-language haikus, by William Higginson:

> Holding the water,
> Held by it –
> The dark mud.[9]

I am reminded too of David Abram's notion of the 'reciprocity of the senses', that everything we touch in order to make it known to us also touches us and somehow knows us.[10]

John Teasdale is less ecstatic, more pragmatic, than James Agee. And David Abrams. But even so, there is something galvanising and a little atavistic in the intimacy with ancestors that is evinced in John's footage. With his modestly devotional cinematography he shows how he understands that everyone can be streamed inward upon, how everyone must make a life while being bombarded by the enormous sleeting of objects, forms and ghosts.

This avidity, this devotedness, why not call it by its name? It is a kind of love. And it can be brought to the centre of the investigation. In doing so, I will call on two guides. The filmmaker Roberto Rossellini. And the esteemed historian Donna Dening, Greg's widow, writing under the name of Donna Merwick.

Drawing from Donna's work first, from her enthralling book *Stuyvesant Bound: an essay on loss across time*, she reminds us that the people in the past have always 'lived with mysteries' and have habitually 'constructed representations of the supernatural', just as we citizens of late-capitalism and globalisation live mystified nowadays even if we rarely admit so.[11] Donna elaborates, explaining how people from the past—for example the earliest Dutch colonists on Manhattan—'seldom operated along strictly rational lines of procedure', for 'they were prey to swings of emotion—ambition, the desire to earn natives' approval and "engineer morality", working out feelings of inadequacy, disloyalty, indifference, or repugnance at their own cruelty'.[12] And if we are to know anything from examining the traces these people left, we need to think through those oozing affections.

This is a good moment to reprise Raymond Williams: we need to examine 'social experiences in solution'.

I can supplement Donna's insight with Rossellini's memoir entitled *My Method*, in which he tries to define what makes great realist art: '[You must follow] someone with love', says Rossellini…'[you must watch] all his discoveries and impressions… What is important is the waiting…and the love.'[13]

It is the same with traces from the past, I think. It is what leads us to the 'shapener' who is *in* and *of* the world. It is mud holding and held by water. It is Abrams touching the world and being touched by it. It is Greg Dening's conviction that history requires an extravagant slowness, a patient layering approach, and a trust in a kaleidoscopic, roundabout mode of apprehension.[14]

So we are back with 'Greg Dening Precept No. 3' exhorting us to seek and to know with the entire sensorium, emotionally and aesthetically as well as linguistically and rationally. I confess that I have just added that term 'aesthetically', but I trust Greg would permit me, especially if we insist on the original and the best connotation of 'aesthetic': 'that which is perceptible by the senses'.

Which brings us back to Joris Ivens and to the theme of *connectedness* that John Teasdale lets us see and helps us feel in his footage. I hope it has been evident in all the imagery I have shown: this sense of an animating force of *relatedness* that brings real significance and vivacity to the world that human beings try to parse and tend.

As I conclude my remembrance of Greg Dening's legacy, I am reminded again the observation in one of Stephane Mallarme's letters, where the poet declares that because there are already enough objects in the world—there is no need to invent new things—all we need do is create new relationships among the things that already exist.[15]

This urge to *relate*—to move through a shifting, pulsing experience that delivers truth as an experience that is close and deeply *felt*: it is evident in John Teasdale's work. It is evident in Greg Dening's work too. The urge to relate is an attentiveness to the pulse of all experience. It is something felt like yearning, like a connection to some vital quality quickening the world.

So, to finish our archival imagining for now, I insist that this urge—this yearning to relate—is something intimate and motivating that can abide across time, across spaces, across cultures and across realms of being—across realms of being human, animal, vegetable and mineral. It is the reason for doing the work—this urge to show and know relationships across cultures, space and time. It is the obligation with which we are blessed when we work with the remnants of the past. And it is the most wonderful thing, extracted from the plenitude he offered, that I learned from Greg Dening.

Notes

1   G. Dening, 'Performing Cross-Culturally', *The Australasian Journal of American Studies,* 2006, vol. 25, no. 2, p. 5.
2   Dening, 'Performing Cross-Culturally', pp. 2–9.
3   O. Grober, *The Mediation of Ornament*, Princeton University Press, 1992, p. 227.
4   Interview with Anne Carson in the online magazine *UNSAID* http://unsaidmagazine.wordpress.com/2012/09/11/gifts-and-questions-an-interview-with-anne-carson-by-kevin-mcneilly/, accessed 20 September 2014.
5   R. Williams, *Marxism and Literature,* Oxford University Press, Oxford, 1977, p. 132.
6   Williams, p. 133.
7   See E. Michaels, *For a Cultural Future: Francis Jupurrurla makes TV at Yuendumu*, Artspace, Malvern, 1987.
8   J. Agee and W. Evans, *Let us Now Praise Famous Men*, Houghton Mifflin, Boston, 1988, (first published 1941) p. 110.
9   W. Higginson in C. van den Heuvel (ed.), *The Haiku Anthology,* Simon & Schuster, New York, 1986, p. 88.
10 D. Abram, *The Spell of the Sensuous: perception and language in a more-than-human world*, Vintage Books, New York, 1997.
11 D. Merwick, *Stuyvesant Bound: an essay on loss across time,* University of Pennsylvania Press, Philadelphia, 2013, p. 83.
12 Merwick, *Stuyvesant Bound*, p. 160
13 R. Rossellini, *My Method: writings and interviews*, Marsilio Editori, Venice, 1987, p. 63.
14 Dening, 'Performing Cross-Culturally', p. 5.
15 S. Mallarmé, 'Reponse a Jules Huret', *Oeuvres completes,* Gallimard, Paris, 1961, p. 871.

ACKNOWLEDGMENTS

The writing in this book has been sustained by an academic culture, mainly in Australia but also reaching out to the rest of the world, that is dedicated to the rigorous review and encouragement of everyday culture and the work of imaginative thinking. Because of the strictures and the sense of obligation and responsibility pressing upon everyone working in this context, you could call the culture an economy, so long as you realise how much dedication and generosity goes into it, dedication and generosity beyond the simple measures and evaluation of economic accounting.

I am indebted to many people, institutions and publications for their support, especially for the editorial improvement and dissemination of early drafts of many chapters in this book. I acknowledge and thank them here. If I have missed anyone, the error is inadvertent and the gratitude abides.

Versions of chapters appeared in the following publishing entities:

Ashgate Publishing
Australian Humanities Review
Cultural Studies Review
History of Photography
Journal of Material Culture
Melbourne Historical Journal

MIT Press
Monash University Publishing
Memory Studies Journal
Rethinking History
Rouge Online Journal
Tate Modern, London (Publications Unit)
Transformations Journal

I owe special thanks to the following people:

David Carlin
Donna Dening
Adrian Martin
Shane Strange
Susannah Radstone
Laurene Vaughan
Graeme Were
Jonathan Walker
Jen Webb
Terri-ann White

Most of all, as always, I thank Kathryn Bird.

www.ingramcontent.com/pod-product-compliance
Lightning Source LLC
Chambersburg PA
CBHW020648220526
45464CB00001B/342